JOSH T. C. EVERETT

The Edge of the Dark

A Guide to Surviving Suicidal Thoughts

First published by Josh T.C. Everett 2026

First edition

This book was professionally typeset on Reedsy.
Find out more at reedsy.com

Contents

Introduction

One day a boy woke up and decided to kill himself. Some time later, a woman he met took scissors to her wrists. This is the story of how they got there and how they escaped.

This book is meant to help you either survive suicidal thoughts or help someone who you believe may be considering suicide.

It pulls from decades of research across millions of people to give you the knowledge and resources to make survival more possible.

In Part One you will learn how to help yourself stay alive in the fight against suicide. You will learn how loneliness, sleep, screens, exercise, diet, and purpose all play a role in making us want to live—or not. Once you see the impact these levers have on your mental health, you will be given tools to push or pull them as you choose to bring yourself to a better place. In reading this book, you will be given actionable steps, based on the best scientific data we have, to help. The tools in this section will give you the best chance of beating this thing.

Part Two is about helping others. It includes data on suicide and mental health, discusses why people kill themselves, shows you how to identify if someone is having suicidal thoughts, and gives you tools to help them as best you can—a challenging, but not impossible, feat.

If you are struggling with suicidal thoughts, I recommend reading this book from beginning to end. You'll find the actionable steps summarized at the end of each section for your convenience.

If you want to help someone who might be struggling with suicidal thoughts, I recommend starting with Part Two so you can be equipped with the knowledge and know-how to help. Once you've finished Part Two, Part One may give you a deeper glimpse into the feelings and thoughts of someone who is in distress, or how they can improve their own mental health.

If you are in immediate danger, call emergency services (911 in the U.S.) right away. If you are considering committing suicide, call or text the Suicide Lifelife at 988. They are available 24 hours a day and they can help.

I

Helping Yourself

1

Escaping the Road to Death

No one is born wanting to die. For most of our lives, we would fight tooth and nail for the next breath, kicking and screaming, doing whatever we can to protect the flame of life. We will hunt for the fountain of youth, hope for technology, pray that God will save us. Death is the final enemy.

Until one day it isn't.

Maybe it's because there's something in our lives that hurts so much we can't bear it. Maybe it's because for some reason or another, continuing to live feels impossible. Maybe we feel like there are no other options, like hope has died, like this horrible moment will just never end. We stop seeing any way out that involves us surviving. Death goes from being the enemy to being the escape. Suicide begins to feel like the only option.

We dress this up in a word that sounds like a drug you'd get from a pharmacy: "Suicide." The murder of the self, the killing of potential, the end of all that could be. The end of all points where we could turn back.

The road to suicide is hell. So why do some people walk down it? It isn't often voluntary. No one wakes up and *wants* to want their own death. Even those who desire their own end often wake up wishing that they wanted something better, that they loved themselves more. Suicide is often a sort of last resort, the culmination of pain and trauma to the point that survival stops feeling possible. The pain that leads to suicide is different for everyone, and it can feel like you're the only person in the world who knows what it's like. The pain could be depression or anxiety, a mental illness, trauma or stress, loneliness, poor physical health, a loss of purpose or hopelessness. It could just be that you're tired and ready to go. Suicidal thought is the body's way of telling you that something is hurting so much that it is killing you. Something must change; something has to go, whether it is the circumstances or you.

This leaves us with a glimmer of hope. If suicidal thoughts are the body's way of telling you that something has to change, then this means if you can change things, the thoughts can go away. Change can reduce suicidal thoughts.

For some people this feels impossible. It is not.

It can be difficult, but there is a light at the end of the tunnel. For many people, this light is going to be finding someone to talk to. Just having someone to listen to you seems to stop a huge number of suicides—a study of 437 adults by the Columbia University Irving Medical Center found that 98% of people who called a suicide hotline said that it helped them, and 88% said that it stopped them from killing themselves.[1] For others, the way out will be to make small changes in lifestyle—changes that those burdened by the weight of suicide *can* make—that have been shown to help the majority of people. For some, the changes might be more dramatic, the flip-the-tables and burn-the-ships kind of change that helped some of the survivors in this book escape death.

The road to suicide is hell, and getting off it is hard, often harder than continuing as you are. Many never find the way off, and some of those who do won't take it because even in pain, a new path can be more frightening than the one we're on right now, the devil we know more comforting than the devil we don't. Don't alow yourself to be one of these people.

You deserve to live. You won the battle against the overwhelming odds of the universe when the atoms that make you all found themselves in one place, when the unbroken chain of your ancestors survived harsh reality and formed you. You are a miracle.

You can make a positive impact on the world around you. No one else in the entire universe is exactly where you are right now, in your exact situation, with the genetic makeup and experiences you have. No one else can do exactly what you can do from where you're at. You can be a gift to the universe.

You hold immense power to make your dreams come true, and because of your uniqueness, no one else will have the exact dreams you have. We live in an age when almost anything that can be imagined can be achieved. You are not stuck forever; your future is malleable, and your dreams achievable. This can be a gift from you, to you.

I promise you: you can change. The way out may be painful at times. It can be scary, and getting from where you're at to a better place can seem impossible, but this book is meant to help you get yourself to a better place. Change is easier than the road that leads to self-destruction. If you are considering suicide, please call the suicide hotline at 988. They will listen to you. You may also continue reading. Below we will talk about how you can save yourself.

2

Friends

Being alone will kill you.

Loneliness is perhaps the greatest single driver of suicide, and one of the most consistent risk factors for depression. While compiling the Survival Stories at the end of this book, I found that loneliness played a part in *every single one* of the survivors' suicide attempts—and that fixing loneliness by building deep connections, decreasing screen time, and even finding their life's purpose created a positive chain reaction. Fixing loneliness is the first step in improving a lot of things in life.

But loneliness is getting worse: In the past there were fewer walls, less distance between neighbors, few ways to communicate other than face-to-face. It is only in the modern world that we can replace real connection with screens, work from and deliver food to our homes without ever leaving, pass entire days speaking to almost no one.

All of this has led to a staggering rise in loneliness, especially among younger generations. A 2023 poll from the American Psychiatric Association found that about 30% of adults over the age of 34 have felt lonely at least once per week over the past year, and 30% of 18–34 year-olds have felt lonely *every day.*[2]

There are several things that contribute to loneliness, but a few stand out: A 2024 survey from Harvard's Marking Caring Common Project found that 61% of lonely people said they don't have enough close friends or family, 67% felt they weren't a part of any meaningful groups, and 73% felt like technology contributed to their loneliness.[3]

Mia, whose story you can read in Survival Stories, had often felt lonely—her father and brother were abusive, she had few strong friendships, and she felt more comfortable with screens than with people. But her boyfriend was a shining light for her, a safe space. She pictured them living together in a foreign country. She dreamed of joining the military just to be closer to him. He seemed to be so different, so *right.* Mia had often felt lonely, but almost never *alone* until the day that they broke up.

Plans, gone. Future, blurry.

The breakup caused Mia to spiral: Loneliness seemed to sap her energy and she stopped exercising. Her money problems all of a sudden seemed worse than they were before, and were exacerbated when her brother started demanding money from her. She wanted to numb her mind, so she turned to screens—movies, reels, anything that could take her mind off the present situation. Her social life soured until it was worse than ever, and got so bad that Mia's only living connections were her cats. Even her mom lived far away and could offer minimal support.

So Mia decided to get in her car, drive onto the nearest train tracks, and wait. Lack of connection wasn't her only problem, but it was the one that was going to kill her.

Building connections would save her. In the moments before Mia cranked the car she thought of her mom, far away, who Mia supported with her own money. She thought of her cats who would go to live on the streets and perhaps die to dogs, if they didn't die of hunger first.

Mia got out of her car and walked back inside. She lived, improved, and to this day is still getting better. She's building more connections, making more friends, even dating again. Loneliness took her to the edge of the dark, and connection brought her back.

Loneliness is the gateway to the path of pain, both in Mia's story and in an abundance of research. The same survey by Harvard's Marking Caring Common Project found that 81% of lonely adults felt depressed or anxious and 75% said that they felt no meaning or purpose. The authors of the study wrote that, "While loneliness can certainly induce and deepen anxiety, depression and feelings of meaninglessness, these feelings can also induce and deepen loneliness."

In other words, loneliness leads us down a slippery slope, a downward spiral, causing negative feelings that, in turn, make you feel more lonely. The worse you feel, the worse you can get, and the harder it becomes to pull yourself out. This loneliness causes us to spiral, so let's call it the Spiral of Misery: This tendency for bad feelings to make us feel even worse, and for escape to feel further away.

But there is good news, too: The Spiral of Misery has a good twin that we will call the Cycle of Better, in which doing even small good things for yourself can cause other positive emotions, which, over time, can lift you out of misery. Reducing loneliness will be the first step off the Spiral of Misery and into the Cycle of Better for many people.

Reducing loneliness can feel daunting, in part because loneliness is subjective. According to Harvard's study referenced above, some people feel loneliness because they lack friends and family. Others might have friends and family, but no deep connections they can rely on (if you ask Americans how many close confidants they could discuss their life and decisions with, the most common answer is "zero.")[4] Some people feel loneliness from not having a purpose, and others from feeling like they aren't a part of their own country.

There may be many kinds of loneliness, but there is one cure for almost all of them: A supportive friend who you can share the little details and big decisions of your life with (as opposed to a "shallow friendship" whom you might see around town, but don't have much familiarity with). Friends who you can spend time with, who you can vent to, who can keep you company, who can save your life. Supportive friends are perhaps the strongest protection against loneliness, depression, and suicide.

The quality of friends you have matters more than the quantity. Research by the University of Pennsylvania shows that the ideal friend is trustworthy, honest, supportive, fun, and someone you can see in person, preferably on a regular basis.[5] Having a supportive friend has been shown to be particularly powerful: A meta analysis published by the Frontiers in Psychology journal looked at over 70,000 individuals and found that having a supportive friend is linked with one's emotional wellbeing and can protect against depression and loneliness. The researchers found that out of all the traits a friend could have, supportive-ness predicted higher levels of well-being more than any other variable. Having this supportive friend put people on the path to the Cycle of Better. Researchers in the study write,

> *"When friends interact within a positive emotional atmosphere, their experience broadens and this, in turn,*

> *activates an upward spiral which evokes even more positive emotions..."*

The study also found that there's something unique about having a good friend, something that isn't captured in any other kind of relationship.

> *"Although individuals could reap the benefits of friendship from other social sources as well, it became evident that friendship is a special type of relationship, with a unique contribution to wellbeing."*[6]

Having this friend could save your life. And not having this friend could kill you–a meta analysis by Brigham Young University and University of North Carolina at Chapel Hill looked at over 300,000 people, their health, and their friendships and determined that not having strong social connections was as bad for your health as smoking, worse than obesity or not exercising.[7]

So how does one find supportive friends? It starts with making up your mind. Research by the Universities of Manitoba and North Dakota shows that friendships don't just happen, they have to be *made*. Believing that friendships will just pop up for you is correlated with higher levels of loneliness five years later. On the flip side, the simple belief that "making friends depends on effort" is correlated with lower levels of loneliness.[8] Just believing that you must make friends to have friends will take you from a passive friend-finder to an active one—and it is what you need to believe to beat your loneliness.

Once you believe that you must make your friends, the next thing to do is stop avoidance. There are two kinds of avoidance:

overt (like when you avoid going out to meet people) and covert (like when you avoid talking to people when you're out). Both kinds of avoidance make it almost impossible to make and deepen friendships. Making friendships requires getting out in new places and talking to people. For introverts, this may sound about as pleasant as cleaning all the hair out of all the shower drains in the world. But research shows that the more you are friendly with other people, the friendlier they are with you. A study by the University of Helsinki looked at a classroom of students and asked them how welcoming or unwelcoming the class was. The students who engaged with other students rated the classroom as friendly and welcoming. The students who kept to themselves rated the classroom as unwelcoming.[9] If you're scared of being sociable, it may help to remember: Everyone wants friends just as much as you do, and most people are just as scared as you are to be sociable. By being social with others, you might can help save them from loneliness, depression, and even suicide.

Once you have made up your mind to start making friends and being social, it's time to start showing up to places. People will begin to like you more just by seeing you often–unless you just stand, glowering, in a trench coat–through what is called the *mere exposure effect*, a cognitive bias that makes us like things more when we are exposed to them often. You don't have to be a social butterfly, perfect diplomat, or have people clapping their knees with your jokes. You just have to show up, and the more you show up, the easier it becomes to socialize.

The ideal places to show up are places where you will have fun. The goal here is to find a good person or good people (supportive, honest, trustworthy) who you can hang out with a lot to get the maximum benefits of friendship. So start with your current interests, then broaden the search if no one good turns up.

In Survival Stories you can read the story of Matt, who, after contemplating suicide as a teenager, survived, and as an adult moved to a city where he didn't know anyone. He started to feel lonely soon after arriving and decided to try out different activities to make new friends. He went to a Meetup.com hiking group, started going to boxing classes, and trained for a triathlon. He met a lot of new people in the hiking group, but didn't really connect with any of them. Boxing classes were a lot of fun, and he started building some budding friendships, but most of the guys there were *really* into boxing and not much else (Matt was mostly into other things and not so much into boxing). For his triathlon training, he started swimming, biking, and running, but didn't have much luck finding groups that did any of these things on a regular basis or at the pace he liked. All in all, he tried to find groups in many of his existing hobbies and didn't have much luck. It was time to branch out.

Matt had always watched dancers with a certain envy—why was he born with Latino desire and Caucasian ability (which is to say, not much)? His favorite dance move was the one where he hid in a corner and hoped no one invited him to dance. But Matt always thought it would be fun to learn how to dance, so he signed up for an intro salsa class. He thought he was the worst one in the class, but there was some potential. Between stumbling and stepping on toes he met a lot of people. He decided to go back the next week.

He met even more people when he returned. "I apologize in advance for my skill level at this," he told his partners every time he danced with someone new. Two of them thought it was funny, or that Matt was a sad little thing, and invited him to another dance class after, an advanced class, a new style to add to his growing repertoire of moves. "I haven't taken the intro class," Matt told them, "I don't think they'll let me in."

"Just try it," one of them said back to him. "We'll keep your secret."

For a moment Matt stood almost frozen, brain rushing to find excuses so he could avoid the class and go home. *It's getting late,* he thought, *I need to go to bed* (it was almost 8pm). *I haven't taken the intro, I'll be the worst one there* (but he was already the worst one in his salsa class, and it was a lot of fun). *I'll embarrass myself* (no doubt about it, but this was still just an excuse). He walked toward the doors where the class was and opened them to a bunch of spinning people in cowboy–and cowgirl–boots blaring country music. He *did* embarrass himself, and he was the worst one there, and he was a little late to bed. But after class, several of the dancers told Matt how happy they were to have him there, asked for his number, and invited him to a group chat. That week, he went hiking and had lunch with people he met in the class (and was invited to go dancing at a bar, but it was past his bedtime). Matt went to the bar a few weeks later and had the time of his life. One of his dance friends later turned into his absolute best friend in the world, and they're now planning a trip to Costa Rica together. As a lifelong lonely person, Matt never imagined that it would be so *easy* to make friends just by expanding his own hobbies.

You, too, can try something new if you've had trouble finding friends who share your interests. Keep trying new things until you meet people who you would be happy to hang out with again and again. You might be surprised, as Matt was, to find that your new hobby is even more fun than your old hobbies. It just takes some courage to get started.

Summary of Friend Finding

- Making friends is perhaps the biggest single defense against loneliness, depression, and suicide
- The modern world makes us lonely
- The ideal friend is someone who is kind and supportive, honest, trustworthy, shares similar interests, and is physically close (so you can see them often)
- Making friends is active, not passive. You have to make it happen
- If you're having trouble making friends in your current hobbies, try new ones

3

Sleep

Ricardo was the king of bad sleep. His childhood was often spent going to bed with the television on or playing video games until he couldn't keep his eyes open any longer. He went to bed late, tossed and turned during the nights, and woke up early. His room was often hot bordering on hellfire, and loud, with the sounds of his family nearby. It's probably no coincidence that the most depressing moments of his life were those when he was sleeping the worst. He considered killing himself when he was at a point where most people would have thought that he'd "made it": He was in his early 20s, earning money in dollars (a rarity in his country), and had recently purchased his own home to remodel.

"The house was kinda a mess and wasn't ready to stay in," he told me in an interview for this book, "so I was staying in a nearby apartment, the smallest one I could find so I could save money and afford the contractors for the renovations. I shared it with cockroaches, and it was so small that when I went to sleep, my head was in the bedroom, and my feet were in the kitchen," he laughed.

Ricardo didn't have problems with the size of the apartment he was staying in, or even the little beings he shared it with. Among crippling loneliness while taking on this renovation project, a story detailed in Survival Stories at the end of this book, Ricardo's poor sleep got worse. He would wake up early in the morning to work, spend time at the renovation project managing contractors, running errands, or getting supplies, and then would work again until late at night. "It was a constant cycle," he told me. "Wake up, work in front of a screen, work at my house, work in [front of] the screen again, then bed." But bedtime was not as relaxing as it should have been. Ricardo's apartment sat at the edge of a forest and the cicada calls rang loud. The summer heat made the room stuffy and hot, and Ricardo had no air conditioning. He had trouble sleeping in the heat and often woke up in a bed damp with sweat.

"It was horrible," he remembered, voice low and quiet. "I could feel it affecting my brain. That time in my life was the only time I ever considered killing myself. Bad sleep wasn't the only reason—it made a lot of bad things at the time worse—but it was definitely part of the reason I wanted to end it."

If there is a hall of fame for protecting against depression and suicide, making friends would have the number one spot of all time. Getting enough sleep would be a close second.

Research shows that people who sleep less are more likely to get depression, and people with depression sleep less.[10] It's the Spiral of Misery all over again. "It's becoming increasingly clear that sleep and mood have a bidirectional relationship," said Andrea Goldstein-Piekarski, PhD, assistant professor of psychiatry and behavioral sciences and director of the Computational Psychiatry, Neuroscience, and Sleep Laboratory at Stanford Medicine.[11]

We aren't exactly sure *why* sleep has such an impact on mood, only that it does, and in a big way. Ricardo is not the only one who suffers with poor-sleep blues; the research we have shows that poor sleepers are 2.5× more likely to have frequent mental distress, which could be anything from depression, anxiety, or stress, to other psychological illnesses, all of which increase the likelihood of suicide.[12]

Poor sleep is nefarious because it doesn't just affect how we feel, but affects what we *do*. Research shows that sleep-deprived people start to lose their ability to think long term. They start thinking short-term, start taking more risks,[13] start losing their fear of losses and seeking more short-term solutions. A study by the Department of Psychology and Neuroscience at Duke University found that sleep deprived individuals were more likely to pursue "high-risk behavior by being disproportionately incentivized toward reward-seeking while concurrently being desensitized to ongoing losses." In other words, people who sleep less stop caring so much about what they are losing.[14] Impaired long-term thinking, increased risk taking, preference for short-term solutions, and the desensitization of loss all form the perfect storm for someone who is thinking about suicide, a step down the Spiral of Misery.

It doesn't take long for the effects of bad sleep to begin ruining your life. One single night of poor sleep can cause you to make worse decisions and become a worse problem solver,[15] and the effects can compound over time. If you have poor sleep, you are a prime candidate for suicidal thoughts and actions. If suicide was a person, a panther, a real life monster, it would be on the prowl for those who don't spend enough time sleeping and those who get poor quality sleep on a regular basis.

You can know you're one of the poor-slept if any of the

following is true:

- You aren't sleeping at least eight hours a night in a cool, dark, quiet room
- You are going to bed and waking up at different times on a regular basis
- You feel like you could nap or doze often, such as while watching TV, reading, on devices, driving, or talking to someone

Getting perfect sleep probably isn't possible; getting good sleep is often challenging enough. But it will make a difference in your mood. Here's how you can sleep as well as possible:

Screen Be Gone: The first step is to limit your screen time, especially near bed. Phones in particular are a true menace to those who wish to sleep (though tablets, computers, and television are all harmful, too). Phones are so impactful on sleep that even daytime use causes nighttime sleep issues. A study by the Rawalpindi Medical University looked at 280 medical students to see how their phone usage impacted their sleep. Like most other med students, the students at Rawalpindi were probably working hard, studying a lot, and had extra incentive to let their minds recover with a good night's sleep. They probably *had* to sleep well just in order to get through med school. But even for med students, who have every reason to sleep well and sleep often, the study found that any phone screen time over two hours per day was associated with poorer sleep than med students who had less time with their phones. (In case you're one of the people who doesn't think you use your phone that much, the same study found that people tend to under-report their usage times.)[16]

Excessive screen time during the day is bad, but screens at night are a nightmare. One study showed that cutting off blue light (the kind that comes from screens) two hours before bedtime was so powerful that it improved clinical insomnia.[17] Adding a blue-light filter on your phone or turning on bedtime mode might help, but the best bang for your buck will be to get rid of screens altogether. Having at least two screen-free hours before bed seems to be the sweet spot, but research has shown positive impacts on sleep just by turning off screens thirty minutes before bed.[18] Lowering your screen usage during the day, and especially at night, will improve your sleep.

Running After Z's: The second step to great sleep is to move more (sorry for all you exercise-haters, but this will come up again later). If you exercise, you will sleep better. It doesn't even seem to matter what kind of exercise you do; multiple studies show that you can improve your sleep by doing activities from walking, gardening, swimming for fun, and yoga to sports, lifting weights, and martial arts. In other words, it seems like almost any imaginable physical activity will help you sleep. And you don't need much of whatever you're doing: Research shows that as little as thirty minutes per day can help you sleep better.

Consistency is the most important factor. In an ideal world, you should be doing some kind of movement every day. Some days might be more intense than others (lifting weights, biking, running, etc.) and some more relaxed (a nice hike or walk through the park). The point is just to keep moving, elevate your heart rate, breathe a little harder, and feel tired after.

Timing your exercise with your sleep also matters. It's best not to exercise too close to bedtime (within three hours or so) since this raises your core body temperature and prevents you from cooling enough for sleep.[19,20] If you are a fan of late night exercises, then you can cool your core temperature back to a sleep-friendly level by taking a hot shower after your exercise... which you should probably do anyways.

Your Room: Your environment can be one of the biggest barriers to excellent sleep. Humans sleep best in a cold, dark, quiet place with no predators present (some of those criteria might be more important than others).

Your bedroom might be too warm for you to rest well. According to the Sleep Foundation, the ideal bedroom temperature for sleeping is 65–18 for our more rational, international friends.[21] The Sleep Foundation also says that rooms should be "as dark as possible" and that the closer we get to bedtime, the more we should be dimming our lights and turning off screens (don't get mad at me for bringing it up again).[22] Your cool, dark room should also be quiet. And before all the fan-sleepers come at me with pitchforks, it seems like sound *variation* is as important than sound *intensity*: Sleeping in a quiet room with occasional blaring sirens or street-side shouts is worse than sleeping in a room with a low-level constant noise. Fans, rain sounds, white noise, or other consistent noises are fine, and can even be protective if they're drowning out variable noises from the outside. The goal here is to get your room as quiet as possible with as few disturbing sounds as possible, so try playing around with different strategies (like noise makers, ear plugs, or melting your neighbor's saxophone) and find what works for you.[23] It's worth taking some time to organize your sleep environment.

Ricardo's sleep improved when he moved out of the stuffy, loud apartment he shared with all sorts of critters. His new room, in his remodeled home, had air conditioning, was quiet, and guarded against all manner of crawling things. "I started having the best sleep of my life," he told me.

Consistency: You will sleep better with a consistent bedtime. Don't shoot the messenger—I, too, love to stay up late watching movies, playing games, hanging with friends, and procrastinating bedtime because after sleep comes work, and work is no fun. But a consistent bedtime is going to do as much for your sleep health as just about anything else, including cutting out screens, exercising, and sleeping in a good environment. In general, it's best to go to sleep and wake up at the same time every day. It doesn't seem to matter much *when* you wake up and go to bed (though earlier might be a little better); it matters far more that you wake up and go to bed at about the same time every day.[24] Congratulations, your new sleep goal is to sleep like a grandpa.

Catching Up: If you do have some nights of poor sleep, try your best to catch up. This could mean taking a nap during the day or giving yourself more time to sleep the next night. Research is split on whether you can "catch up" on your sleep, but it seems obvious that we *can* catch up, at least a little. Miss a night of sleep and your body will be craving rest the next day. Naps in particular have been shown to help you in all the ways that a regular night's sleep help: Boosting energy and improving mood are two relevant effects for our purposes.[25]

Whatever the research says (and just to be clear: by and large the research supports napping, hallelujah, blessed be the word), your body will let you know when you're not sleeping enough. Don't fight it. Try to catch up if you can and, if not, make it a point to establish good sleep habits in the future.

Before we move on to the next section, it's worth mentioning that oversleeping is sometimes a *symptom*, not a *cause* of depression. According to the Cleveland Clinic, the way to combat oversleeping is, in part, to be consistent with your sleep schedule, to get light during the day and turn off artificial light at night, and to go to bed early enough that you don't have to use an alarm or the dreaded snooze button.[26] If you find yourself sleeping too much–such as over nine hours per night–it is probably worth investing in your sleep quality. Following the steps in this section will improve your sleep quality, and help both those who sleep too little and those who sleep too much.

Summary of Sleeping Well

- Cutting out screens before bed
- Moving daily
- Sleeping in a cool, dark, quiet place
- Being consistent with your sleep schedule
- Catching up and taking naps or sleeping longer the next night

4

Screens

If friend-finding and sleeping have the top two spots in the Depression-Defending Hall of Fame, then screen time would bring up third. You've already seen how screen time can impact sleep, but it seems the problem runs deeper than that.

According to the Pew Research Center, the overwhelming majority of people across a wide slew of countries believe that their phones make a significant improvement in their lives, that mobile phones are good for society in general and good for them personally. Most people in the research said that their phones free them, save them time, and a significant portion of people said that they couldn't live without their phones.[27] Perhaps it's because phones make it easy to connect. Across all of human history it has never been easier to get reviews of a business, shop around before buying, and call Mom.

Mark Zuckerberg, CEO of Meta, wrote a public statement talking about the benefits of Facebook soon before they became a publicly-traded company. He mentioned how Facebook could help the global economy by giving people more opinions about businesses. He said that Facebook could help empower democracy by making peoples' voices heard, bringing about a more transparent dialogue between people and government. He said that Facebook "creates a more open culture and leads to a better understanding of the lives and perspectives of others." Zuckerberg was writing about Facebook, but all of this could be said about screens in general: Phones, computers, television could all be argued to increase connection, increase visibility, increase voice. But is it true?

Real-life friendships start with real-life connection. A conversation, a smile, a "Hey, can I ask a question?" Screens seem to be getting in the way of us making these connections with new people and maintaining them with existing relationships. Researchers in a joint study by Georgetown University, University of British Colombia, and the University of California, Irvine looked at what they called "absent presence": the tendency of people to be physically present but mentally absent from a situation. Imagine being somewhere like a waiting room, the gym, a sports game, and people are on their phones instead of paying attention to the world around them. This is absent presence. Researchers in this study asked whether phones increase absent presence and prevent us from approaching others, stopping us before we can even make eye contact and smile with someone.

Their findings won't surprise you. Participants in the study who were without their phones smiled more, had more genuine smiles, and were more approachable. They didn't have absent presence, just presence. Researchers wrote that "participants with smartphones exhibited significantly fewer smiles of any kind" and concluded that phones form a significant barrier to forming new connections with real people.[28]

New connections are not the only ones at risk. Another research group from Princeton University and New York University also determined to find out what damage phones are causing to our existing real-world relationships. The researchers asked people what they thought when they were spending time with someone who brought their phone out during the time together. The researchers then asked people to rate things like enjoyment, engagement, and connection in the social interaction. More phone use had a strong connection to less enjoyment, less engagement, and less social connection. What might surprise you is that almost everyone said that their own phone usage didn't affect social relationships, but other people's phone usage did. In other words, we all think it's fine when *we* pull out our own phones. It's when others pull out their phones that we start feeling that it's hurting the relationship. We have a blind spot to ourselves; we don't realize the damage caused by pulling out screens while with other people. The researchers concluded that

> *"phone use in social situations can increase feelings of exclusion, decrease relationship satisfaction and relationship quality in romantic relationships, and lower overall life satisfaction. Our studies provide evidence that some of these negative effects can extend to platonic relationships as well. If people continue to use their phones, not recognizing that it impacts their partners in the same way their partner's phone use affects them, we could end up in a "phubbing loop" that results in mutual relationship dissatisfaction."*[29]

While with others, put the phone down and turn the screens off.

Screens are bad when they're causing you to brush off other people. They also don't seem to make you much happier if you're using them while alone, though the science gets murky. As best we can tell, technology use is fine until it starts to interfere with other, more important things, such as being present with other people, going outside and getting sunlight, getting to bed on time, working, or being physically active.[30] But it's ever harder to put the devices down. They're everywhere, always on, designed to addict us.

Social media seems to be the grand offender. In a 2024 senate hearing related to youth mental health, Mark Zuckerberg, now CEO of Meta (who owns Facebook, Instagram, WhatsApp, and more) said that "it's important to look at the science, and the bulk does not support that [social media causes mental health issues]." His statement was met with widespread disbelief. "You have a product that's killing people," one senator commented.[31]

The science seems to agree with the senator. People who use social media often are almost twice as likely to have depression, three times as likely to have a negative view of their own body,[32] and significantly more likely to commit suicide, especially when usage interferes with sleep, relationships, or lowers self-esteem. Research by Florida State and San Diego State Universities found that high social media use was associated with higher risk of suicide than even unemployment.[33]

Mitchell Prinstein, chief science officer of the American Psychological Association, looked at the studies provided by Meta's CEO to support the claim that social media doesn't have harmful negative effects. His conclusion was simple.

> *"Zuckerberg cherry-picked data to suit his purposes... Social media is related to psychological harm through online discrimination, prejudice, hate and cyberbullying. Research also has found that young people face serious*

> *risks when they are exposed to content about self-harm, harm to others, or eating disorders."* [34]

Some of the research Prinstein is referring to has shown how social media usage can begin benign and work its way down to outright bad. A user might start watching exercise videos, then get exposed to content about dieting, then about eating disorders, then about how to enable yourself to lose extreme amounts of weight in unhealthy ways. Content looking at clothes might lead down the rabbit hole of better-and-better-looking people in those clothes, people who seem godlike in their beauty, unreachable from where you're at. Content about depression can spiral into content about self-harm, suicide. Worse, research by the University of North Carolina at Chapel Hill has shown that we begin to imitate the kind of content we consume. Those who consume alcohol-related content will often start drinking more. Those who see content about depression, self-harm, and suicide will often fall deeper down the Spiral of Misery.[35]

These are some extreme cases and won't happen to everyone, but now more than ever the pressure is on *us* to make sure that these things don't consume our lives. We are fighting against armies of software engineers, psychologists, and CEOs who want us to spend more and more time on their platform. Even if you can avoid the extremes, the low-severity, more common outcome is the one in which social media simply takes up too much of your time, depriving you of sleep, family time, hurting self-perception and self-esteem in subtle ways, and keeping you from healthy activities like exercise or being outdoors.[36]

Some research indicates that it's a problem of quantity, how much social media you're using. Prinstein disagrees. "The potential for harm is baked into Facebook, Instagram, and other social media platforms if [used] as intended... This problem will not be solved by limiting access to these apps on mobile devices. Real change requires modifying the features and functions of the social media apps themselves... to prioritize psychological health more than making a profit."[37] According to Prinstein, quantity doesn't matter if the quality is bad enough.

The bulk of the evidence seems to support that screen use is fine as long as it's kept in control and doesn't interfere with other areas of your life. Don't let it keep you from sleeping, keep you from talking, keep you from connecting with the real world around you. Social media is probably fine in small doses, but those doses should be kept as low as possible.

With the risks as high as they are, and the rewards as low, the burden of proof is on you to show that social media isn't harming you. The default assumption should be that it is.

If you are going to use social media, avoid doomscrolling and assume that what you consume will consume you. I recommend setting app timers to kick you off after a certain period of time, or even deleting the app every time after you use it. Social media is made to keep you coming back and spending more time on it, so be careful and use an abundance of caution. If you're in doubt whether social media is harming you or not, it's probably best to turn it off.

I deleted all of my social media in my early twenties and the difference in my mental health was almost immediate. The world became more interesting; I stopped comparing myself and people around me to the images I would see on a screen. I had so much *time* all of a sudden. If you figure we have eight hours of work, eight hours of sleep, eight hours of free time, and we're spending two hours per day on social media, that's *a quarter of all our free time.* What would you do with an extra two hours every day? Would your life be improved?

As someone who has no social media and has everything blocked, I recommend cutting it out for a week, a month, and seeing the impact it has on you. My guess is you'll feel a lot better and not miss many of the "positives" that social media claims to have.

Summary of Screens

- In general, screens are fine, but after a few hours per day, more screens means more depression
- Overusing screens so they interfere with other aspects of life seems to have the worst effects. About the time when you start skipping sleep or social outings to watch a screen is about the time you should turn them off
- Social media's pros probably don't outweigh the cons. If you're going to use it, consider limits. Assume that what you consume will consume you, and will change how you view the world
- Try turning social media off for a week and see how you feel. Consider having one day per week where you don't use your phone at all

5

Exercise

Suicidal thoughts will not improve if you lie in bed all day. An Italian meta-analysis from the University of Milan and University of Rome looked at fifteen different studies spanning hundreds of thousands of people and concluded that "physical inactivity is a pandemic."[38] Connection to people, sleep, and disconnection from screens will all have enormous impacts on your mental health. Exercise will, too. And if you're looking to feel as good as possible in the shortest amount of time, exercise might be more impactful than anything else.

In a study of over 150,000 people, researchers were able to tie low activity levels to higher levels of mental anguish such as depression and anxiety. Participants who scored low in cardiovascular and strength tests were twice as likely to have depression and 60 percent more likely to feel anxiety. Senior author Dr. Joseph Hayes said, "Our findings suggest that encouraging people to exercise more could have extensive public health benefits, improving not only our physical health but our mental health too."[39]

This presents us with a problem. By definition, depression

may present itself as "decreased energy or increased tiredness or fatigue." In plain English, depression may manifest itself as *not working out.* There's no study looking at how many depressed people feel too depressed to work out, but my guess is that *all* depressed people have felt too blue to break out a sweat at some point or another. While composing Survivor Stories at the end of this book I found that *all* of the people I interviewed have been so depressed that, at times, all they wanted to do was lie in bed and hope that tomorrow would be better—preferably with an whole pint of ice cream.

Perhaps there are some people who can muster up the willpower and *just do it* and go for a run or lift heavy things or do whatever exercise means to them. Maybe there are some who can just discipline-and-pain their way out of depression. But there are many who can't. As with almost everything we've talked about so far, the Spiral of Misery is at work: The less we exercise, the more down we get. The more down we get, the less we want to exercise.

There are two ways out of the Spiral of Misery and into the Cycle of Better. Researchers have found that when it comes to exercise and poor mental health, you can improve *either one* to improve the other. A study titled *Feeling Too Low to be Active* looked at 9,900 people and found that "Mental health interventions may generate spillovers in physical activity and health."[40] In other words, if you are stuck in the Spiral of being inactive, being inactive causing you to feel bad, and feeling bad causing you to be inactive, then you can improve your physical health *or your mental health* and one may start spilling over into the other. For the person who feels too bad to be active, a solution may be to do the other things we've talked about (improving relationships, sleep, screen time, (and soon diet), then leverage mental health benefits to start exercising. Goodbye Spiral of Misery, hello Cycle of Better.

If you *can* stand to do some physical activity, then almost any will be better than none. Hippocrates, of Hippocratic Oath fame, is believed to have said "Walking is man's best medicine." Modern science has found some evidence behind this idea when it comes to mental health. Remember the Italian study looking at hundreds of thousands of people that called physical inactivity a pandemic? The same study found that people were able to reduce the total number of depressive episodes by 25 percent if they exercised three times per week.[41] And this isn't vigorous, Navy-Seal-style training that'll make you want to curl into a fetal position and cry in the corner. It seems that even a little walking can be good enough.

The World Health Organization recommends about 150 minutes of exercise, or about 75 minutes of vigorous exercise per week. This totals out to about 20 minutes per day of activities like "recreational or leisure-time physical activity, transportation (e.g walking or cycling), occupational (i.e. work), household chores, play, games, sports or planned exercise, in the context of daily, family, and community activities." In other words, pretty much anything that isn't sitting down can help depressive moods, giving you the mental space to be more active.[42]

Twenty minutes per day might be the recommendation, but studies find that even less movement will have some beneficial impact. The meta-analysis from Italy writes, "Even below the recommended levels, small doses of physical activity can gain mental benefits and are associated with lower risks of depression."[43] It doesn't seem to matter much what you do, just that you do *something*.

If you have the energy for it, there seems to be extra benefit in doing an exercise that will get you breathing harder, and for exercising more than the minimum. The same meta-analysis above showed that people with low cardiovascular fitness had a 64 percent higher chance of having depression. Steven Ball, associate professor of Nutrition and Exercise Physiology at the University of Missouri, writes that, "some [exercise] is better than none, more is better than some, and too much is hard to get."[44] But the best exercise of all will be one that you stick with.

Matt had been lifting weights since he was a teenager and always enjoyed the feeling of finishing a tough workout (a habit that may have saved his life in high school), but nothing compared to the joy of running for him. He loved turning on an audiobook and taking off into the hills to catch good views, running for hours, multiple times per week, not pursuing fitness, just wanting to be out in nature. Then his knee started hurting. He kept running, and it kept hurting, then it started hurting more. For the first time in his life, as a man in his twenties, he went to physical therapy. The knee seemed to get better before getting worse again. In a panic, Matt scheduled an MRI that found he had extreme damage to the cartilage of his knee. It was irreparable. He was devastated.

Doctors told Matt that he may never be able to run again, should definitely cut out hills, and should consider giving up hiking. "Hearing that I shared knees with my grandma was worse than a cancer diagnosis for me," he told me in our interview. "I told my boxing coach that I'd rather hear I had six months to live than give up running and hiking." Matt added that boxing coaches are far cheaper than therapy.

Matt had some hard days after that diagnosis, but he decided that he would make a way through it. He gave up triathlon training, trying to preserve what function remained in my knee.

Without running or hiking, he had to take up new exercises to stay healthy. Matt already knew from triathlon training that he hated biking and swimming, so Matt decided to start dancing. There was a studio not far from him teaching salsa, bachata, and a few swing dances. He started by learning the basics, then learning how to do spins, spin the other person, how to dip the lovely ladies without dropping them, and more. He started making friends, dancing until he was breathing hard, going out to bars where Matt and his new friends would dance until they closed for the night. Dance became Matt's favorite exercise and social activity after almost three decades of two left feet. He might never have started if it weren't for his knee problem.

If you're having trouble finding an activity you love, then try broadening your search. Anything is better than nothing. If you are in a place where your depression won't allow you to exercise, then either come back to this one when other things have improved (such as friends, sleep, screen time, and diet). Or start small. Walk to the kitchen and back, to the front door and back a few times, to the block down the street, into the woods or park for five minutes. Or maybe try an activity that doesn't *feel* like exercise. For Matt, hiking and dancing don't feel like exercise because he loves them so much. For you, any movement is going to be beneficial, so start where you can.

If you want exercising to have the most impact possible, then opt for social exercises (classes, group activities, sports, etc.) or anything outdoors. These kinds of activities will help you make friends and will get some sun, which can further help with mental health.[45]

Alongside making friends and improving mental health, exercise improves sleep, self esteem, and even social support.[46] It's possible to be depressed when you're healthy, sleeping well, have a lot of social support, and are rocking a six pack. But it's tough. Any kind of exercise can put a larger barrier between you and depression or suicidal thoughts. Pick an activity you can stick with, and try something new if you're not a big fan of movement.

Summary of Exercise

- Exercise improves mental health
- About twenty minutes per day is a good starting point, but it's hard to have too much (though not impossible, as Matt's wounded knee shows). More does seem to be more when it comes to improving mental health
- The best exercise is one you'll stick with. If you're going for the minimum effective dose, do something that will allow you to breathe, but not sing
- If you don't like exercise, maybe try something else. It doesn't have to be a sport or something that looks like torture with extra steps. Try something you think you might like and, if you don't like it, try something else. It took Matt a decade and a bum knee to find his favorite exercise of all (dance)
- For bonus points, try combining exercise with either sunlight or a social group
- Consistency is the most important thing

6

Diet

There's a growing body of evidence that what we eat affects what we think, that what we consume will consume us. If we put junk in, it might not come out. It might go straight to the brain.

Junk food in the brain has been shown to increase depression, anxiety, nervousness, restlessness, lack of motivation, and even stress. The Spiral of Misery rears its ugly head once more; a joint study by the University of Maryland, Baltimore, and the University of Illinois found that poor mental health seems to lead some people to eat worse, and eating worse seems to steer people in the direction of depression.[47] What we eat affects what we think, and unhealthy food leads to unhealthy thoughts. The worst offenders seem to be ultra-processed food, fast foods, unhealthy snacks (like a candy bar or a bag of chips), sugar-sweetened beverages, and excessive alcohol consumption. Avoiding these things can help with your mental health.

Cutting out junk foods will help with mental health, but the benefits don't stop once you cut out cookies. It seems like the healthier your diet, the more likely you are to have positive mental health. The Mediterranean diet, a diet characterized by consuming low-meat, healthy fats such as nuts or avocados, whole grains, and minimal alcohol, seems to be a clear winner when it comes to mental health. A study following over 10,000 people since 1999 indicates that the Mediterranean diet protects against depression[48] and the Cleveland Clinic says it provides other benefits as well: lower body fat, protection against cancer, and even a longer lifespan.[49]

At its core, the Mediterranean diet is about eating natural foods. It has limited sugar intake, trades white grains for whole (including brown rice and whole wheat options), and limits alcohol. The Med diet trades a lot of red meat consumption for fish, especially fish with healthy fats like salmon, anchovies, or sardines, and it promotes high vegetable consumption. Nuts and fruits are safe for eating too.

If your diet is filled with fast, junk, or guilty-pleasure foods, then one simple way to improve your mental and physical health is to cut the junk out. Simple to say, hard to do. Tools like GLP-1s might help, but the jury is still out on whether these weight-loss drugs affect mental health and, if so, how much.

In my experience, good diets are made in the grocery store, not at home; if junk is in the house, it'll end up in the belly. So start your healthy food lifestyle while shopping (preferably shopping after a good meal).

Summary of Diet

- Poor diet is associated with poor mental health, and a healthy diet seems to protect against poor mental health. The better you eat, the better you'll feel
- The worst offenders seem to be ultra-processed foods, lots

of sugar, fast foods, unhealthy snacks, and lots of alcohol. If your great-grandmother wouldn't have eaten it, you should probably avoid it

- The best dietary defense against mental angst seems to be the Mediterranean diet: low-meat, high vegetables, lots of healthy fats from fish, nuts, and some dairy, minimal alcohol
- As the saying goes, abs are made in the grocery store. Shop well to eat well. If junk is in the kitchen, it'll end up in the belly

7

Purpose

Purposelessness and feelings of meaninglessness or hopelessness can lead to suicidal thoughts and actions.[50] This effect is so powerful that just believing in nihilism (the philosophy that life has no purpose) can lead people to consider suicide.[51] What goes on in your head shapes your reality, and not having a reason to be here can lead you to not be here at all. The Spiral plays a role here as well: Purposeless leads to loneliness, and poor lifestyle choices that, in turn, lead to more purposelessness.

On the flip side, having a purpose, can save your life and protect you against suicide (among other benefits). Purpose in life makes people healthier, happier, and live longer.[52] Having something to come home to, a reason to wake up, being someone who is needed, finishing a project of yours, being there for friends and family, doing meaningful work, serving a higher cause, *any purpose at all* is protective; it doesn't much matter what your purpose is, just that you have one.

Even if you do everything else right, maybe *especially* if you're doing everything else right, lacking purpose will make everything else in this book mean less. This is perhaps the foundation of all life, the reason to live at all, the linchpin, the cornerstone. If you feel lost and rudderless, then finding a purpose will be a matter of life and death for you.

But what if you don't have a purpose, a cause, a *something*?

The places to start are with loneliness and sleep. Of the purpose levers you can move to heal depression and suicidal thought (connection, sleep, screens, exercise, diet, and purpose), loneliness and sleep are both connected to a lack of purpose though the Spiral of Misery. One causes the other, and round and round we go 'til we all fall down. Personally, the times in my life when I have felt the least meaning have been the times when I have had few friends or little sleep. To this day, it's the moments when I feel lonely or when I haven't slept well that I begin to question the meaning of it all. If you're feeling a lack of life's purpose, then fixing loneliness and lack of sleep is first on the list.

If you have several close friends and are sleeping well but still feel rudderless, there are a few paths you can take. Choose any, or all if you're an overachiever.

Embrace Challenge: Perhaps the easiest way to have a purpose is to give yourself one. This can be anything that's meaningful to you. The goal here is to find something that's hard, but not impossible. Something you can get done in a certain timeframe so you can give yourself a deadline. Something you can tell someone that you're going to do so you have some social accountability. Here are some ideas to get your brain juices flowing:

- Learn to play an instrument
- Compete in an event
- Learn a new language

- Learn a new sport or martial art
- Travel somewhere you've never been
- Become a better dancer
- Become a better artist, or finish a piece you've begun
- Finish a mile in a certain time
- Write a book
- Achieve a certain weight
- Become a better chef
- Break your personal best in the gym
- Read a certain number of books

It doesn't matter what challenge you choose so long as you have something to look for on the horizon. The trick here is to choose something that you will stick with and is meaningful to you, that is hard but not impossible, with a deadline, that you can tell someone about.

Care For Another: Animals, kids, and care-taking can save your life. A study of 1.5 million people found that having kids reduces suicide rates by 54–93%, an effect that seems to increase with the number of children someone has—more kids, less suicide risk.[53] I'm not telling you to go have kids, but finding someone to care for might be a good idea if you have felt suicidal. It could be a volunteer group that visits elderly people, a religious organization that helps the community, or even a pet of your own. A joint study by the University of Denver, Purdue University and the US Department of Veteran Affairs found that just having an animal companion (whether it's a dog, cat, bird, horse, or other) can lower suicide risk.[54] (You get bonus points for adopting an animal from a shelter where it was going to die or live its whole life in a cage. I am not sure what these points are good for or what you get with them, but I will give them to you.) If you are struggling with suicidal thoughts, perhaps find someone whose life is a lot better because you're in it.

Find A Higher Purpose: This one gets a little weird, and will probably offend you in some way or another, but stick with me. Studies have shown that there's no difference in how often religious and non-religious people consider suicide, or have suicidal thoughts. But there is a difference in how often religious and non-religious people *attempt* suicide, with religious people attempting suicide less. This seems to hold true across cultures and across different belief systems.[55]

We don't know why this is the case; it's not clear what about religion seems to be protecting people. Perhaps it is due to suicide being taboo in most religions, and this keeping some amount of people from killing themselves. Perhaps religious people commit fewer suicides because they have more social support. Perhaps it's because they feel some higher purpose, a holy mission given to them by God, that they don't want to fail. Perhaps it's that, on average, religious people have more children, and *this* is what protects them. It could be all of these things, or none of them.

What exactly is protecting religious people perhaps doesn't matter. Whether it's the taboo or the social support or the purpose or the children. What matters is that none of these factors are exclusive to religion. There is nothing here that you can't have. You can ask yourself why you are here and, whether you hear a divine voice or not, settle on an answer. The answer could be anywhere from raising a family to protecting your nation to seeing the lost reach salvation. It could be helping the disadvantaged, giving animals a better life, researching for the betterment of humanity. The religious person might say the purpose is given by God, the non-religious person that you are allowed to choose your own. For our purposes, it doesn't matter who is right. Any purpose, divine or not, can protect you against suicide.

A good purpose has a few elements. It's something bigger than you, something that can live on when you die. It's something you can make an impact on. It's something you can find allies in.

Matt didn't know anyone when he moved to to a new city. He was out hiking one morning, going up the same mountain where he would soon meet a girl bleeding from her wrists, but this time, on the way down, he saw a group of people picking up trash by the side of the trail. They carried large trash bags, reflective vests, little trash grabbers they used to pick up litter. "Here I am spending my Saturday hiking, and they're making the trail better for everyone," he told me. "I went home and began looking up volunteer opportunities." Many were things Matt wasn't interested in (picking weeds from a farm) or things he wouldn't be much help in (cooking for the homeless, where he would do more harm than good). But one opportunity stuck out. A nonprofit needed volunteers to help teach English to immigrants. On Saturday, they were going for a walk in the park and needed someone to speak to the students. Matt signed up.

The group was mostly Spanish-speakers, and, by chance, Matt was the only one of the volunteers—or teachers—who could speak Spanish. He went from new kid in the group to bouncing around, translating, and explaining things in Spanish when the students couldn't understand English. He was able to teach translations of concepts they already knew in their heads but couldn't voice in English. When they finished our short hike and snack together, the head teacher thanked Matt. "The students really enjoyed having you here. Would you ever like to come back?"

Volunteering became the best part of Matt's week. Other students and volunteers became his first friends in his new city. This one little purpose—helping immigrants learn English—allowed Matt to help the world, find friends, and start making a home in a new place. It all worked to make Matt perhaps the happiest he had ever been. "I would call my parents, and they would tell me how happy I sounded," he said, eyes watery. He paused to rub the tears away. "One time we were calling, and Dad thought I had hung up the phone. 'You can tell he's happy,' he said to my mom. Then he realized I was still hearing, and we all laughed about it."

Even after Matt's close pass with suicide, and his injury keeping him from some of his favorite activities, his new friendships, new hobbies, new purpose, a higher calling, helped him be happier than perhaps he had ever been.

Choose to live for something bigger than yourself.

Return To Your Childhood: As children we dream big things. As adults we look back and wish our dreams could have come true, but finances, work, studies, life, shackles of the modern world all get in the way. It is easy to become the kind of adult who would have disappointed our younger selves: The kind of adult who is not an astronaut or a hero, who doesn't own a ranch in the middle of the wilderness, who has little hope of ever ruling the world. Many of our younger selves might look at our current life and say, "That's *it*?"

The younger self has almost a divine sense that we lose as we get older, an arrow pointing straight toward our destiny. One way to find a purpose is to open yourself up to this inner voice again, to once again believe that you have a calling to do something in this world. Return to the things that spoke to you when you were a child, the inner sense of purpose, the knowledge of your place in the world. For many this will be reawakening a lost dream: To become an artist, a hero, a parent, an owner. Our childhood often holds the key to our future. Return to whatever called you in those simpler times, and find the path to make your destiny a reality.

Drastic Change: If you've tried everything and nothing is working, then perhaps a drastic change is in order. Here's an example. I was depressed during high school and college, and it seemed to get worse as I got older. I hated my job, gained a bunch of weight (to the point I hated my body), and felt like my path in life wasn't leading where I wanted. The divine fate of childhood gave way to a simple adult reality: money. I could run the numbers and see that I would be working my entire adult life, no hope of retirement before the age of regular colonoscopies (which, in my late teens, seemed impossibly far away), in jobs that were bland on Fridays and soul-sucking from Monday to Thursday. *There has to be more*, I kept telling myself. Life felt empty.

My internal strife started becoming external. I broke up with my girlfriend, started dreading work, dreading college. There didn't seem to be a "common sense" answer to my problems. The worldly wisdom of those around me stopped at "Grow up, get a job, get married, have kids, live in debt, die." It never answered questions like how to be happy. *What if I wasn't? What do I do then?* I saw the slow death I was dying.

Perhaps it was divine aid that helped me make the next step, or maybe I was just an animal, cornered by life, willing to do anything to make it to safety. I took my life savings and booked a three-month ticket to Costa Rica and a few months in an Airbnb. Common sense didn't approve of *that*, nor did all the worldly wisdom of those who loved me and meant well. The best evidence I have for the existence of Good and Evil is that almost by chance, a boy from the boonies of Georgia with no bright future changed everything for himself by making a bold decision to improve his future. I saw then that my options for life were to accept the way it was going to be, to work to change it, or to leave it. I chose to change it. To this day I am amazed at my own bravery at taking my future in my own hands. As a child, I had dreamed of tying balloons around my waist and popping them to fly to China. The Good showed me how to return to that dream.

I didn't know anyone after I hopped on the one-way flight, didn't speak the local language, had never been before. It was a complete reset, a new start from zero, a clean slate.

Strange things happened. Despite not speaking the language, I found it easier to make friends. I wasn't working out at all other than walking, but I lost weight. I had no direction, no end goal, no final destination in my trip or in life (a big change for someone who was always a type A planner), but I found that I didn't need all this anxiety for the future. I got laughed at almost every day while learning the language and making rookie mistakes, and I found it easier to laugh at myself. Life started seeming easier. During my trip I learned things about myself that I hadn't seen for two decades.

This was and remains one of the happiest times of my life, with some of the most memorable moments and best stories. The trip wasn't perfect; I got hit with a bout of loneliness about halfway through, had to hitchhike through near-jungle, and getting laughed at every day took a toll, but it started a chain reaction in me. I had never realized that I hated the place where I grew up and lived most of my life—hated the lifestyle, the culture, even the food. Location wasn't the source of all my self-loathing I felt throughout life, but location wasn't guilt-free either. The dramatic shift in my life—the decision to leave everything and move abroad, the jump in the abyss of the unknown–made me a better person.

I cannot imagine a version of myself that never moved abroad, that stayed in the situation I grew up in for the first two decades of my life, and survived.

When I think of all the good things in my life—my current best friends, my health, my hobbies, my talents, my work, the girls I loved, this book—all of them come from that first dramatic change. The escape.

There aren't any studies saying that this is the right thing, the thing you could or should do to escape a future where you kill yourself, but it helped me. If you look at your own future and see a version of yourself that doesn't survive, then maybe it's time to make a dramatic shift. Maybe you're in a situation where that doesn't seem possible: You have kids, or expenses, or are afraid for one of a million other reasons. I'm sure all of that is true, and it will be more challenging for you to make big changes than it would be for someone in their early twenties with no commitments and no responsibilities. But if you believe that you might not survive the future, then you may have no other choice. It is a matter of life and death. You need a change.

I don't know what this change looks like for you, but I believe that right now you can hear a small voice inside you telling you what needs to go, what mountains you must move in order to be happy. It doesn't have to be as dramatic as a move to another country, but could be something like getting out of debt, improving your health, making friends, escaping abuse. All of these represent different ways to fight back against the hunger of shadows, the ever-encroaching darkness.

If you aren't sure where to begin, then start with friends and sleep. Invest all your energy in building connections with others and in recovering well at night. Next, trade screens for moments outside, for real-life hobbies. Become active if you're able to tolerate it, and trade junk food for whole food. Find a purpose. If you don't have one, then here is one to start:

Live to see tomorrow.

For additional resources on how to survive suicidal thoughts, continue to the Resources & Emergency Help section on the next page. For stories of others who have faced and survived suicide, continue on to Suicide Stories.

II

Helping Others

8

About Suicide

In 2023, 12.8 million people in the United States seriously thought about killing themselves. Of these 12.8 million people, 3.7 million made a plan to kill themselves, and 1.5 million attempted it. This means that if you met 1,000 people in in 2023, 40 of them thought about killing themselves, 10 of them made a plan to do it, and 4 of them tried it. A total of 49,000 people died of suicide in the United States in 2023, or about 1 every 11 minutes.

Suicide is one of the world's leading causes of death.[56] If you take 1,000 people from around the globe and put them in a room, about 13 of them will die from suicide. This is more than the number of people who will be killed by war, terrorism, and homicide *put together.*[57] Suicide is not particular about whose life it takes, but some groups are more at risk than others. It targets all age groups, but is the second leading cause of death for ages 10–34, and people over 85 are more at risk of suicide than any other age group. Suicide takes men and women, but men make up about 80% of all suicides. Suicide targets all ethnicities, but Native Americans, Whites, and Pacific Islanders attempt suicide two-to-three times as often as any other ethnic group. Suicide targets all occupations, but veterans, miners, and construction workers are at higher risk. Suicide doesn't care who you love, but young people people who identify as lesbian, gay, or bisexual have higher rates of suicide. Some groups are more at risk than others, but suicide is the enemy of us all.

Suicide causes lasting and widespread destruction. For every one death by suicide, there are 10 emergency room hospital visits for self harm. The emotional impact is incalculable.

Suicide is getting worse. Suicide rates have increased by 36% since the year 2000, though trends vary by year, age group, and region. More people are killing themselves than at any point in history both in absolute numbers and in percentage of the population. In other words, this problem is every bit as bad as can be imagined.

But lives can be saved.

Why Do People Kill Themselves?

People commit suicide because they feel their life is no longer worth living.

There are a lot of reasons they might feel this way. It could be some kind of trauma: physical, emotional, mental. It could be some kind of loss: job, marriage, loved one. It could be situational: lack of connections, exercise, purpose, poor sleep, or poor diet. It could be biological: mental illness or genetics hindering a person's happiness. Any of these things could lead to suicidal thought or action.

Suicidal thought is the body's way of saying that something has to change. The status quo isn't good enough any more; something is hurting. Suicidal thought is the final call for help.

It does not mean that suicide is inevitable. It does not mean that the person experiencing the thoughts has somehow failed.

Those who are thinking of suicide will often, but not always, have changes in their lifestyle that we can view as further calls for help: They might start being reclusive, quit hobbies, take mind-numbing actions (such as a lot of screen time), engage in risky behavior. They might stop caring for themselves and may begin to hurt themselves on purpose. As discussed in Part One, these behaviors often increase feelings of depression, anxiety, and suicidal thoughts in what we call the Spiral of Misery. It seems counterintuitive; if a person feels bad and if the body is trying to escape some kind of pain, why would it engage in behaviors that make it feel worse? Why would it stop good activities and start bad ones?

Getting out of this Spiral of Misery alone is possible, but hard. Someone who is having suicidal thoughts, who stops socializing, who starts engaging in risky behavior, who stops their hobbies, is sending a signal to the world:

I need help getting out of this.

9

Helping

People who attempt suicide often give some sort of warning sign before killing themselves.[58] Some of these have been discussed earlier in this book, but here is the full list in one place for your convenience:

Previous Self-Harm: Perhaps the best predictor of suicidal thoughts and actions are previous attempts to self-harm in any way.

Negative Talk: Saying things like how they want to die (even in jest), talking about feeling alone or empty, saying people would be better off without them, giving what feels like a final goodbye. This talk can be negative toward themselves, such as "the world is better off without me," or can also be negative in general, such as "I don't see the point of living."

Impulsive and Damaging Behavior: Actions like risky driving, drug use, binge eating, or other behaviors that expose oneself to risky, scary, or harmful situations indicate that the individual may be contemplating suicide.

Mood Disorders: Hopelessness, depression, anxiety, narcissism, antisocial behavior, paranoia, schizophrenia, and many more mood disorders are all tied to future suicidal behaviors.

Parental Relationship: The evidence on this one is still emerging, but it seems that a poor maternal relationship is predictive of future suicide attempts.[59] Research is still inconclusive on a poor paternal relationship's affect on suicide, but we can speculate that a poor paternal relationship would also be predictive of future suicide attempts.

Loneliness: Social connections are a strong shield against mental anguish. Someone with low-to-no real life social connections is more likely to attempt suicide. Connections behind a screen count for something, but not as much as a friend you can walk, talk, and eat with.

Poor Sleep: Not sleeping well (either in quantity or quality) makes the brain go haywire. Someone who is not getting a consistent eight hours of sleep, who uses an alarm on a regular basis, who sleeps in a loud, hot, or bright room will be more likely to have suicidal thoughts.

Lots of Screen Time: Screen time seems to drive mental anguish. At high doses, when the virtual world takes over the physical on a regular basis, screens and media seem to drive destructive behaviors. It is called "doom scrolling" for a reason. There are many pathways to pain when it comes to screens, but the most common ones are things like:

- Seeing content about self harm, depression, suicide
- Using screens so much that they keep you from building real-world relationships, sleeping, or exercising
- Creating self-esteem issues

Lack of Exercise: The stationary body is more likely to develop depression and suicidal thoughts or actions. Almost any kind of movement is better for mental health than just sitting, and the activity doesn't need to be long or painful. A simple walk will help, but more is probably better.

Poor Diet: Junk in stays in. Diets high in sugar, fats, or that are highly processed with few nutrients all have negative impacts on mental health. While shopping, any food without a label (meats, fruits, vegetables) is probably good. Tearing the label off of ice cream doesn't count.

Lack of Purpose: Lack of purpose could be caused by a loss of someone important, losing a job, or not having much of a reason to wake up in the morning. This one is hard to solve, but even a small step in the right direction is better than none. A new hobby, a pet, any reason to wake up in the morning is helpful.

How You Can Help

Listening is perhaps the most powerful thing you can do for someone considering suicide. Both the National Institute of Mental Health and the 988 Lifeline recommend asking a person you believe to be at risk: "Are you thinking about suicide?"[60] Evidence suggests that having open, honest, vulnerable conversations about suicide may reduce suicidal thoughts,[61] which lines up with all the evidence we have about connections being a strong protector against suicide. Being there for someone, listening without judgment, hearing their pain can help an enormous amount. The 988 Lifeline recommends that you "be willing to listen. Allow expressions of feelings. Accept the feelings. Be non-judgmental. Don't debate whether suicide is right or wrong, or whether feelings are good or bad. Don't lecture on the value of life." Just listen. Ask questions. Keep them safe.

The National Institute of Mental Health recommends removing anything that could be lethal or could be used to attempt suicide. You can't block every possible way of attempting suicide, but you can make it as challenging as possible. This is often enough.

If possible, try to connect the person with the 988 Lifeline by calling or texting 988. Having a trained professional listen and offer guidance can be helpful; a majority of people who called the lifeline said that it helped them, and contacting a mental health professional such as a therapist might also help.

Keep in touch with the person you're trying to help. Stay in regular contact with them. This regular cadence will help them see that someone does care, that their life means something. Keep asking about their thoughts and plans for the future.

Suicidal thoughts are the mind's way of saying that something is wrong. Often, this something is one of the factors above. If you are able, find out what's missing, hurting, or unhealthy in that person's life and offer help without forcing it. Your plan doesn't have to be perfect. It can't be. Do the best you can and follow the five steps:

1. **Ask**. "Are you thinking about suicide?"
2. **Be there**. Listen without judgment
3. **Keep them safe**. Remove easy access to the means of suicide (sharp objects, weapons, pills, etc.)
4. **Help them connect** to mental health professionals, including the 988 lifeline
5. **Follow up** and ask again

10

Resources & Emergency Help

Reaching out to a crisis line is great when you're overwhelmed. Trained counselors are available around the clock and conversations are confidential.

In the United States:

- 988 Suicide & Crisis Lifeline: Call or text 988 (available 24/7)
- Crisis Text Line: Text HOME to 741741

International resources:

- International Association for Suicide Prevention: https://www.iasp.info/resources/Crisis_Centres/: A directory of crisis centers in over 50 countries
- Findahelpline.com: A searchable database of helplines worldwide

Make a Simple Safety Plan

A safety plan is a guide you create in advance for moments when distress becomes overwhelming. It will help you survive by following steps you've already determined to do. A basic safety plan includes:

1. Warning signs: What thoughts, feelings, or situations signal that you're heading into crisis?
2. Coping strategies: What can you do on your own to get through a difficult moment? (for example, taking a walk, listening to music, breathing exercises).
3. People and places that provide distraction: Who can you spend time with, or where can you go, to take your mind off things?
4. People you can ask for help: Name two or three people you trust and feel comfortable calling when things get hard. Call these people.
5. Professionals and agencies to contact: Your therapist, doctor, or a crisis line number.
6. Making your environment safer: See the section below.

A free, guided safety planning tool is available at Stanley-Brown Safety Planning (https://suicidesafetyplan.com/wp-content/uploads/2024/12/Stanley-Brown-Safety-Plan-05-02-2024.pdf) or through the MY3 app (iOS and Android).

Means Safety

Research shows that reducing access to lethal means during a crisis saves lives. Even a small barrier between someone and lethal means can provide enough time for the crisis to pass.

- Consider removing weapons and sharp objects from the home.
- Consider storing medications—including over-the-counter ones—with a trusted person, or in a locked box.
- Talk with people close to you about this. Asking for help with means safety can save your life.

You Are Not Alone

Recovery is possible. Many people who have experienced suicidal crises go on to live full, meaningful lives. By reading this book, you have already taken the first step to get to a better place. I believe in you, because I used to be in your shoes, and now I've had the privilege to write a book that you're reading. You have helped my dream come true, so let me speak from experience:

Things can get better, as they have for the people in the Survival Stories section.

If you are in immediate danger, call emergency services (911 in the U.S.) right away. If you are considering committing suicide, call or text the Suicide Lifelife at 988. They are available 24 hours a day and they can help.

III

Survival Stories

The following are true stories from people who have survived suicidal thoughts. Some stories include descriptions of blood, implications of violence and assault, and other distressing themes, but I have tried to keep this section tame enough that I would let my mom or grandmother read it. Please do not continue if you think that stories of people considering suicide will cause you distress in any way. This is your warning: Continue at your own risk.

11

Ricardo

Ricardo's parents thought he'd made it when he purchased his home, in cash, in his early 20s. Ricardo was quick to downplay the achievement in his conversation with me. "It was an ugly house in a small town in a second world country, so it's not as impressive as it sounds," he admitted. "Real estate there is dirt cheap."

But it was his space, and the day he signed the dotted line for it was the first time his parents had ever considered him a man. Before then, he had been something of a rebel: taking a single year of college before leaving, travelling, working odd jobs online, staying single. "We were raised in sort of a strict house. No drinking, no drugs, no girls. My family had never travelled more than a few kilometers from their home, so they were really scared when I started going farther and farther away. I was the black sheep of the family."

Ricardo remembered the conversation when he told his father that he wasn't going back to college. His dad stopped the car, looked Ricardo in the eyes, and said, "I'm just afraid you won't amount to much."

A year later Ricardo joined an online company as a salesman. Another year after that and he was the top rep, earning as much as both of his parents put together. Ricardo saved all the money he could, living in Spartan-levels of minimalism. "Everything I owned could fit in a backpack until I bought a house," he told me through a grin. His parents still seemed to think he was some sort of vagabond.

It was when he bought his house, using all his savings, that his dad pulled Ricardo in for a hug and whispered in his ear, "You're a homeowner. You're a man now."

Ricardo disagreed with his dad's point of view but hurried to defend it. "In his time and culture, home ownership is everything. You have to own your own place. Renting is viewed as less."

But owning caused Ricardo countless problems. The house was ugly and needed major repairs. Ricardo struggled to set up utilities. He hired contractors so he could continue working on his regular job, but caught them stealing from him. Progress improving the home was slow and his split focus caused him to earn less than ever in his job. Funds were getting low, and Ricardo had to rent a nearby apartment to be away from the construction noise so he could focus on his sales job. As detailed in Part One, his sleep started to suffer. His work had to be done in early mornings and late nights when the contractors weren't working on the house, so he woke up early and stayed up late. When he did sleep, the apartment was often too hot and loud for him to sleep well.

Worst of all was the loneliness. His hobbies took a back seat to the house and work. He went weeks without seeing his family, didn't have friends in his new town, and his only people he talked to were the contractors working on his house. "I felt like I couldn't trust anyone, and no one was helping me. It was too much," he said to me. For the first time in his life, Ricardo considered suicide. "I thought about what he would be like for someone to just find my body. It would feel like relief."

During this time Ricardo gave himself a purpose: finish the house. "I kept telling myself the sooner that it was finished the sooner this would all go away and I could get my life back." He paid his contractors extra on days that they seemed tired so that they'd know he valued them. He started learning new skills on the job site so he, too, could work on his home and speed up construction. He asked for help from people in the community when he didn't know how to do something, and they took a liking to the energetic young man who was now their neighbor. They started to pitch in when he needed extra hands or advice on building.

Ricardo went on long walks when he felt overwhelmed. These were the only times he felt he could clear his mind, and the exercise left him feeling better. "It was the only thing that kept me sane," he remembered. Ricardo tried going to the gym as construction progressed, took less of his time, and his frequent shopping trips for materials lessened. But the gym wasn't quite the right fit. He didn't talk with anyone there and didn't love lifting weights, so he stuck with his long walks in the mornings and evenings.

Ricardo's journey to getting better started when the home was livable, construction noise less and less by the day, and his mom came to visit. Beyond helping with clean up—a constant battle in the best of construction sites—she gave Ricardo a social connection. He was able to decompress, to tell her about his day and problems, and she would listen and offer solutions. They laughed together, worked together, and "there's nothing in the world like being a grown man and having your mom make your breakfast. It's the best feeling in the whole world," Ricardo said. His mom was there when he paid the contractors for the last time. "The relief was incredible. No more renovation. Just done," he smiled, memory still fresh. The house, now complete, felt like his.

Having that major stress off his back improved Ricardo's estimation of his own lifespan. The future looked brighter. Now in his own, quiet home, Ricardo started to sleep better. His output at work improved. He had more time for hobbies and friends again, and made many new friends in his new town. He found new routes for his long walks. He stopped considering suicide, though he noted to me that depression can arise again whenever he doesn't sleep well or goes long periods without being near friends. His initial brush with suicidal thought seems to have left a mark; what he had never considered before buying the house now sometimes pops up in his mind. "Some things leave scars," he said.

Ricardo insisted to me that he felt great as long as he was with friends on a regular basis, sleeping well, and walking. It was only when one of these worsened (often causing the others to worsen) that he started having dark thoughts. He still lives in his home as of the time of this book, and noted to me that he loves it, and his community, more than he ever has before. Things aren't perfect. But they are better.

12

Mia

Mia wanted to die, in part, because of her dad. "All he did was be angry all the time and throw hands," she told me in an interview for this book. "He was super patriarchal and allergic to touching a broom... [but] ironically, he didn't even provide for us." She didn't attend his funeral when he passed away. Instead, she felt relieved.

Her family problems were not over. Her brother had learned from her father and began to act in similar ways, forcing the women of the house to serve him. To add insult to injury, Mia told me that they had "zero" money on a regular basis. She herself was always one paycheck away from poverty. With her abusive family and the lack of money, Mia told me that "growing up in such an environment, I always wanted to die."

But she hid it well. To others, Mia was kind, bubbly even, quick to crack a joke and witty in every sentence. During the interview for this book, she told me that one time her niece asked Mia why she seemed so happy all the time. "People around me never even see me frowning," she told me. Few people could have met Mia, energetic and excited, and realized that behind that exterior was a lifetime of pain. Mia is unique in this book because of how long her period of pain lasted, and how well she hid it from others.

Mia continued surviving, in part, because of her mom. Mia realized that if she killed herself, her mom would be devastated. How would she continue on? What would she herself do with her daughter gone? During Mia's interview for this book she remembered asking her mom, jokingly, if she too wanted to die. Her mom said no. Life was a blessing, and all she wanted to do was watch her children have a better life than her own. "That's when I decided I'm going to live longer than her," Mia told me.

Mia's boyfriend was another bright spot in her life, a strong connection that seemed to hold all the other pieces together. "He's the best thing that ever happened to me, and all the plans I made were basically revolving around him," she said. "I saw myself living in a country I don't like just so I could be closer to him." She pictured herself joining the military with him. She was devastated when they broke up.

Mia handled the breakup, the family stress, and money problems well. She continued on. But the final straw happened at work, an event so minor that in hindsight she couldn't even remember what it was. "Something about work stressed me out, and money was tight, but I still had to find a way to help my older brother pay his debts," she said in an interview for this book. No single thing was too much, but all of it together was overwhelming. Mia stopped wanting to get out of bed. She stopped eating and admitted to me that diet, sleep, and exercise "are the things I hadn't been paying attention to." She didn't have deep friendships who she could call and tell everything about her life. Mia considered suicide.

"I was so lost. I didn't know what to do. I had no one to vent [to], let alone to ask for help. It was like three something in the morning when I walked into my car and thought of driving to the nearest railway crossing and waiting for a train to hit me." Mia sat there, alone. She couldn't start her engine. She was afraid. What if she didn't die immediately? What if she was saved and found? "It'd be so embarrassing," she joked, witty humor rising even in the face of such a topic. Worse than the embarrassment, her newly-adopted cats wouldn't have a home, Mia's mom would be devastated, and her family might lose their only income source. "If I died, there would be no food on the table," she said.

Mia got out of her car and went back inside her house. She was alive for the time being, but the pain was not gone, only shoved into the deep recesses of her mind. She had lived, but nothing had changed.

So Mia started making things change.

She made a list of all the things that make her feel better when she's down: hot showers, driving, shopping, movies, journaling, things she could do to stave off bad feelings. These things might not make her feel better long term, but often provided just enough of a short term benefit that they could get her from day to day. When things got bad, she could turn to one of the things on the list to get her mind out of the Spiral of Misery.

Mia exercised more often, became a gym regular, wore out the cardio equipment. She got a personal trainer to help her five days per week, and saw improvements in her body in just two weeks. She admitted to me that it was difficult to start a regular routine, but that going to the gym was more helpful for her mood than anything but her favorite exercise, "the devil's tango."

The stress of being one paycheck away from homeless had gone on too long. Mia started saving money, not allowing her brother to use all her own funds. This had an immediate impact on her mood. "I would have a bad day and look at my bank account and feel safe," she said. Financial security went a long way in reducing her day-to-day stress and cleared her mind.

Mia built more relationships: her cats had kittens, and Mia kept many of them. She started going on dates, though it was challenging to find someone who wanted the same things as she did, and she found many of these short-term relationships unfulfilling. Instead of investing more of her time in shallow connections, she worked on deepening her family relationships by moving back in with her mom. This no doubt had some impact on her love life, but helped her be with someone who loved her, who listened to her, who wanted the best for Mia.

Mia's changes were about as dramatic as one can be without quoting all of Hamlet. Her improvements were as well. She started to feel better after all of these improvements, and each one gave her the energy and desire to continue improving. She was on the Cycle of Better.

Not every day was perfect; a lifetime of pain wouldn't be fixed in weeks, months, or perhaps even years. But life seemed brighter. The future started to look possible. Hopeful. When this book was in the final editing stage some time after my initial interview with Mia, I texted her to ask the last time she had suicidal thoughts, she replied, "I don't know what is going on with me, but I've been sitting here for the last thirty-five minutes wondering why can't I remember."

Her message to those suffering from suicidal thoughts is this: "Keep going. Hold on a little longer because time really does heal."

13

Matt

As best Matt can remember, the day started normal. He woke up, ate breakfast his mom made, hugged his dad, drove his brother and and himself to the private Christian school they would both graduate from. Matt would walk the halls always carrying his commentary Bible in hand, ready at a moment's notice. He didn't have to open it often. He knew all the stories by heart, all the most popular verses and many unpopular ones. He read it every night before bed, seven chapters a night, at a rate that allowed him to read it from cover to cover twice a year. Matt wrote noteworthy verses in a hardback notebook his mom had given him so that he could memorize them, every night starting from the beginning and going to the end, trying his best not to look at the words but to draw them from memory.

"Bible nerds aren't the most popular kids even in a Christian school. No one ever found me behind the bleachers smooching the head cheerleader," he said during his interview for this book. But in Matt's mind, what other way was he supposed to be? He thought he was doing the most important thing, The Right Thing™, and that others should be taking their faith more seriously. His adherence to this belief, and insistence that others adhere as well, didn't help his social life.

Perhaps it was the late nights and early mornings, the lack of sleep that to this day puts Matt in a depressive funk until he sleeps well again. Maybe it was that he didn't have friends, didn't smooch enough cheerleaders, that he wouldn't build connections because they all seemed so *shallow*. They didn't get him. Maybe it was the screen time, the hours spent calling and texting people who often came to Matt with *their* burdens. At the age of 18 Matt had already talked two people off the proverbial ledge. He was so widely known as *the guy who will listen to you* that he actually got referrals—people passed his contact info to other school kids struggling with mental health (a willingness to help that would one day save someone else's life). Maybe it was due to Matt's frozen-, fried-, or sugar-only diet that kept him far away from anything healthy. Maybe he decided to kill himself because he didn't feel like he had a direction in life. He didn't know what he wanted to do, where he wanted to go. Maybe he just hated where he lived and didn't know it yet.

It was probably all of these things. Lack of connection, lack of sleep, too many screens, poor diet, little purpose other than the Bible. Matt was deep down the Spiral of Misery in a bad way, and getting worse. He viewed the day he decided to end his life as a terrible offense to God. There is rarely a silver bullet to get someone out of the Spiral, though Matt searched for one in the gym. He was religious about going to the gym, heading there almost every day after school to do a grueling weight lifting routine, then run, then do body weight exercises. "Looking back, it was probably a way for me to escape my mind for a while. I figured I would do one last workout on the Thursday I decided to kill myself," he said, choking up, breath shaky, tears down his cheeks. It was a moment before he could continue speaking. "Then I would get home before my parents were home from work, walk into the woods with shotgun in hand, call the police to ask them to find my body, and stick the barrel in my mouth. It felt relieving, having a plan. Finally *I* was the one in control. My life was now in my own hands, and I was going to take it."

Earlier that year Matt had a classmate who died. He told me that he remembered their small class sitting in silence, many in tears that they wouldn't see her again. "I wondered if they would do the same for me. Probably not, but I hoped they would."

While working out, he thought of how his parents would feel, tried not to imagine their pain. It wasn't fair what he was going to do to them. What would this do to his father's career as a pastor? Would the church gather around him in support? Or reject him for his son's final sin? Matt wondered about what his future could have been. The things he would never do.

Perhaps it was the divine, or the Good, or just Matt talking to himself, but he heard a little voice inside of him, quiet, still.

"Live. I love you." At the time Matt thought it was the voice of God.

"No, I don't want to. Let me die," he said.

"Live. Your life is not your own."

Matt sat down and started crying on the outdoor track of the gym. No one stopped and asked him if he was okay, no one offered to help. Though years later Matt would be the one to help someone else, he received no help of his own on that day. He was alone. He and the voices in his head, alone together. Matt began to see possibilities. All the things he could be, the places he could go, the things he could do.

He saw how it wasn't fair to his parents who loved him more than their own life. It wasn't fair to Matt, the future version of him who could achieve his dreams. It wasn't fair to his future that might take a turn for the better if only he'd given it a chance.

"I don't want to live," Matt told the voice. "Please don't make me live."

But in that moment, Matt began to feel love. "Maybe it was a god, an angel, the universe, myself. I don't know. At the time I knew that God had a plan for me, that he wouldn't let me live without fulfilling it. Now I don't know. I think perhaps within us all there's at least some part of us that wants to live, that wants to see our destiny fulfilled. When I had no one to help, I had myself, or the voice, or whatever."

Matt sat for half an hour on that track. Alone, the voice and him. It was enough, for a while. For long enough for Matt to recover. In that moment he decided to live. To live for all the possibilities, the adventures, the things he could do for the world. To live for the people who loved him. To live for the love he could give to the world.

Matt survived that dark day, but things didn't get better in that instant. They took time, and they shifted. Matt had to find another purpose when he stopped believing in—and carrying, his big commentary Bible (though he was quick to tell me that he returned to his faith after some years "as a prodigal"). Soon after, Matt went on to delete his social media, began eating greens, started to sleep better. "It took me years to learn how to make friends, though," he admitted, looking embarrassed. But once he learned how to make friends, after moving to Salt Lake City, he seemed to make more friends than he had time for. He had friends from dance, friends from volunteering, gaming friends. His parents told him that he had never seemed so happy.

"It's been a long time since I've thought about suicide," he said, smiling.

Matt later got the chance to help someone else: the woman with the strange tattoo.

14

Kaitlyn

The sun blazed on the day that the woman with the strange tattoo feared for her life. It was an unfortunate reality in Salt Lake City's Augusts that if you were outside, you were going to get roasted. The heat bounced off the road, cooking Matt as he ran from his basement apartment in an older couple's home ("I liked to tell people I lived in an older couple's basement, they just didn't know I was there yet," he laughed) by the capital building, up the mountain to Ensign Park. The mountain looked bad, and it felt worse: A climb that felt half a degree from straight up, one foot barely in front of the other, chest heaving, face red, sweating rivers. But the view at the top, the one over the mountains and the valleys, was stunning. It was still too early for snow—a moment Matt looked forward to after growing up in Georgia—where they might get an inch per year; one of his fondest memories was being out of school for a week due to the *threat* of snow. His day would come on one cold, rainy day in September when the Utah mountains got their first snow, but for now, the mountains were bare, brown-yellow from the rocks and dirt and green in places where meager plant life could eke out a living in the desert where it only rained a few times a year. The view from the top of the mountain, after the run up was finished, was one of Matt's favorites in the world. Going up had been a treat from him, to him. He couldn't stay at the top for too long. For one the sun was turning him into a lobster and sucking him dry of any ounce of moisture he'd been wise enough to carry. But if he stayed up too long, he'd be late.

The way down the mountain was easy. The far mountains and the valley stretched out in front of Matt, the canyon stooping down to his left where he could sneak peeks between the mansions that were built to soak up the view. He passed a tall, slender woman as he reached the bottom of the hill. She looked up, their eyes connected, they smiled. Hers never reached her eyes. Matt's was probably red and sweaty and made him look insane. *Dang, Utah girls are cute*, he thought, wishing that he had looked a little better. *Maybe I'll see her on another run.*

Matt wouldn't have to wait that long to see Sierra again.

The run down the hill took him down into the canyon, a long staircase transitioning him from one hill to the other. Once he hit the staircase, the run was almost over. He was almost home, where he would shower and put on deodorant and find some clothes that might have gotten the tall girl to like him, and then he'd go out again for the special night.

Matt took the first few steps down when he saw the woman with the tattoo. She was tall, large, hair long, eyes pudgy. Her ratty clothes and the sack she was carrying made Matt think she was homeless. For a homeless person, she must have had plenty of money to pay for the tattoos that coated both her arms in sleeves, designs wavy and indistinguishable. He couldn't help but stare as he passed her on the staircase, him running down, her trudging up. The tattoos on her arms were unlike anything he had ever seen. They looked so *real*, almost like...

Something is wrong, said a voice in Matt's head. *She's crying and...* Adrenaline caused his heart to drop into his stomach. *Those aren't tattoos. It's blood. Her arms are covered in blood.* They passed each other, both of them avoiding eye contact. Matt got to the bottom of the staircase and stopped, looked up. He couldn't see her.

Should I go back?

She probably wants to be alone.

What if something is wrong? It has to be wrong; she's bleeding everywhere.

It's none of your business.

Can I live with myself if I don't check on her?

No.

Matt turned around and sprinted back up the stairs. She was at the top, sitting against a stone wall. Her arms were covered in blood, red-stained scissors held in one hand, phone in the other. Tears rolled down her cheeks.

Matt scanned her arms. The blood covered her from wrist to elbow, but most of it seemed dried. At the very least, it didn't seem to be flowing.

"Hey, are you okay?" He asked her. No response. He reached down, touched her shoulder. "Are you alright?"

She shook her head. "No," she whispered, voice faint. He looked around for help. No one. The tall, slender woman, just over on the other side of the road moments before, was gone. If it weren't for Matt, this girl would have been all alone.

"What's your name?"

"Kaitlyn."

"OK, I'm Matt. What's wrong, Kaitlyn?"

She paused, then whispered: "He said he was going to kill

me."

Red-hot anger cut through Matt. The blood, the scissors. *She was protecting herself.* He glanced down the staircase where she came from. Empty. For now. "OK, he is not going to hurt you while I'm here, okay? Are you in danger?"

No response. Matt heard someone talking on the phone, but Kaitlyn seemed frozen.

"Do you want me to talk to whoever is on the phone?"

She handed it to him without a word. Matt saw someone move in the corner of his eye. The tall, slender woman was back, standing in her driveway as Matt reached down to take the phone. He waved her over.

"What's wrong?" she asked.

Matt dropped his voice to a whisper. "She said some guy wanted to kill her. Can you talk to her? She's got someone on the phone."

The slender woman nodded, crouching to be eye level with Kaitlyn. "Are you alright?"

Matt brought the phone to his ear. "Hey, who is this?"

"This is the suicide hotline. Is everything okay?"

Matt took a moment to stop his voice from cracking. The blood, the scissors... Kaitlyn hadn't been hurt by someone else. She had tried to kill herself. Memories almost brought tears to Matt's eyes.

He snapped his fingers to get the slender woman's attention. She was kneeling, talking to Kaitlyn. She looked up. "Suicide hotline." He pointed at the scissors, still in Kaitlyn's hands. The woman's eyes widened as she understood.

"Let's take these away from you, okay?" she said, placing her hand on top of Kaitlyn's and pulling the scissors from her grip. Kaitlyn didn't seem to notice.

"She's bleeding, and she said some guy was trying to kill her," he said into the phone. "I think we might need police and an ambulance here."

"How much blood is there?"

He glanced at Kaitlyn's arms. They were covered in dark red. "A lot. We need some help."

"Let me put you on hold and we'll get someone out there."

"Thank you." He walked back over to the slender woman. She was crouched next to Kaitlyn, smiling that same never-reaches-the-eyes smile. "They're sending someone," he told her.

"An ambulance?"

"Definitely an ambulance, but I want to get the police out here, too."

She nodded. "I'm Sierra, by the way."

"Matt. Nice to meet you. Sorry it's not under better circumstances."

"Likewise." That smile.

Matt saw someone coming up the stairway from the corner of his eye, the same stairway where he had met Kaitlyn. Adrenaline made time seem to slow. *It's the guy who hurt her*, Matt thought. His heart leapt before he realized it was just woman, sides of her head shaved, climbing the stairs, carrying a sack. She gave a big grin, showing off the gaps where her teeth used to be. She got to the top of the stairs, saw Kaitlyn sitting, Sierra kneeling, and Matt trying not to look like he was causing these girls any problems.

"Is everything okay?" The woman asked.

"She just tried to kill herself. Said some guy was threatening to kill her earlier today."

The woman knelt down beside Kaitlyn. "Honey, I used to be in the same exact shoes. My name is Becca. My ex used to beat me..."

The voice came back on the phone asking for directions. Matt stepped away from the ladies to let them talk, only approaching again to ask Sierra how to get to wherever they were at.

"Alright, police and an ambulance are on their way," the voice on the line told him.

"Thank you."

"No problem. I'll stay on the line in case you need anything."

"Okay." Silence. He looked back towards the girls. Sierra was still crouching; Becca was sitting next to Kaitlyn. *Thank God for Becca,* Matt thought. he stayed back where he wouldn't interrupt the girls' moment, but close enough to see down the stairs in case some man came looking for Kaitlyn. He didn't.

Kaitlyn and Becca were smiling, tears in both of their eyes, holding hands when two cop cars, a fire truck, and an ambulance arrived at the same time. *These guys must be having the mother of all boring days. Not much do to in Salt Lake*, he thought.

Paramedics took Kaitlyn's vitals and bandaged her while the cops asked Matt, Sierra, and Becca what had happened. They told their stories, starting with Matt, ending with Becca.

"I know the guy she's talking about," Becca told the police. "He was in my encampment this morning saying crazy things." She told the police where she had last seen him.

They took notes before one of the cops, a big Hispanic man, turned towards his cruiser. "Alright, I'll go see if I can find him." Another officer was talking with Kaitlyn. With paramedics wrapping her arms and the police taking her testimony, Sierra, Becca, and Matt all found themselves with nothing more to do.

"I don't like telling the cops where I live, but that guy was giving me the creeps," Becca said to Matt when she thought the officers couldn't hear.

"Sorry you had to do that. And thank you for your help. I think you were the hero of the day. I didn't know what to say to her."

"You go through some rough times and you can see it in others. We shared some bad experiences," Becca said.

One of the paramedics walked over. Kaitlyn was bandaged up, on a gurney in the ambulance, on her way to the hospital. "She'll be alright. Got some deep cuts but she'll make it. You all did the right thing."

Becca waved goodbye and started up the hill to wherever she was going before meeting them. Matt turned to Sierra. "It was nice meeting you. Feels like we should be friends after this."

"Yeah. See you around."

Guess we weren't gonna be friends after all. "Yeah."

Sierra walked up the driveway back into her home, Matt ran, then walked down the stairs, then stopped. His legs almost gave out, taking him to sit on the sidewalk. He remembered his own time, almost ten years ago to the day, when he too had almost killed himself, when he had been alone.

Tears blurred Matt's vision as he sat on the sidewalk and remembered. He waited until his voice stopped shaking before calling his mom.

"Hello?" she answered.

"Hey, I'm going to be late to dinner. I'll explain everything later. I love you."

"Alright. I love you."

He hung up.

It was Matt's birthday. He later told me that helping Kaitlyn was the best part of that day, that month, that year. "I don't think I did much for Kaitlyn," he told me, "but I'm glad she wasn't alone."

* * *

A few weeks later Matt got a message on the dating app Hinge. A girl had liked him and sent a message.

"I hope this isn't weird, but did I meet you a few weeks ago when we helped a girl?" The message read. Matt opened the profile, looked through the pictures... it was Sierra. The two exchanged phone numbers, then went walking in the park together, then went out for dinner, then to another park...

Sierra told Matt that she had seen Kaitlyn while out walking one evening. Kaitlyn looked better, happier. She had gotten help. Her arms were scarred; they always would be. But she was smiling when she saw Sierra, and thanked her for her help. Kaitlyn said she hadn't seen the man again.

Sierra worked as a nurse and was taking an opportunity in Asia. She was leaving Salt Lake City only a few days after she and Matt exchanged numbers, and the two said goodbye with a long hug in front of Sierra's driveway. They still keep in touch.

Matt went on to hurt his knee with his many long mountain runs, and pick up dancing, and boxing, and volunteering, as detailed in Part One of this book. He told me that he has lots of friends, sleeps well, avoids all social media, stays active, tries his best to eat healthy, has picked up writing, and that he even found love after Sierra. He said that his parents were right. He is the happiest he's ever been.

Dedication

To Efsun. Editor extraordinaire, maxed out charisma, and Goddess of the Wind.

Acknowledgments

Writing a book takes an army, and this one wouldn't have happened without some amazing people. First off, a huge thanks to Ricardo, Mia, and Matt for sharing their stories. This book is far better because of you all, and I appreciate the tears we all shared while going through these stories to make them book-ready. It is brutal to relive some of these experiences, and you all are heroes.

I would like to thank Efsun Güneri for being the first and most supportive reader throughout this whole journey. Your kind and gentle initial edits, when this book was not very good, turned this into something that I'm not embarrassed to publish.

Robert V.S. Redick also made significant and incredible contributions to help me kill my darlings and remove the parts of this book that were not authoritative, not interesting, or not helpful. Your words of encouragement helped me bring this across the finish line, and I am so excited to read future works of yours.

Melissa Woods helped adjust the tone of the book and helped me remove sections where I was not doing my best work. Your expert grasp of the English language astounds me, and has made this book better. Thank you for removing a lot of my filler words and run-on sentences, and for making this book much better.

Zobia Abir created an incredible cover for the book, and talked me out of a very near miss with a cover that was much less incredible. Thank you for your art and graphic design skill.

Finally, thank you to Ruth Muñoz for your support, listening to me rant about my book on our first date (and all the subsequent ones) and for being the best girlfriend ever. I don't want to imagine my life without you.

Thank You, Dear Reader

Dear reader,

Thank you for the time you've invested in this book. It was my dream to be an author since I was a kid when I spent two or three years writing a thirty-page short story that I first shared with a girl in my 6th grade class. She read the story for a few minutes (that was all it took, and more than the story deserved) before she told me how awful it was. She was right, but I kept writing bad stories for the next few decades. I didn't share them with anyone.

It was when I learned Matt's story that I thought, *I can't keep writing bad fiction and hiding away, I have to write something that would have helped these people and get it out there.* That's how this book was born.

If it has been helpful to you or someone you know, then please consider leaving a review on whatever platform you found this. It helps others find this book. If they don't have the means to purchase it, then the book is available for free at https://open.substack.com/pub/joshtceverett/p/the-edge-of-the-dark-free.

Thank you for helping my dream to be an author come true.

About the Author

Josh T. C. Everett wanted to be an author since he was a kid writing science fiction. He still wants to write science fiction, but hasn't gotten there yet. When not writing, he loves hiking, learning languages, bike racing, and reading.

Please feel free to reach out for any reason at joshtceverett@gmail.com, or follow him on Substack at joshtceverett.substack.com.

Notes

ESCAPING THE ROAD TO DEATH

1 Madelyn S. Gould et al., "National Suicide Prevention Lifeline (Now 988 Suicide and Crisis Lifeline): Evaluation of Crisis Call Outcomes for Suicidal Callers," *Suicide and Life-Threatening Behavior* 55, no. 3 (2025): e70020, https://doi.org/10.1111/sltb.7002

FRIENDS

2 American Psychiatric Association, "New APA Poll: One in Three Americans Feels Lonely Every Week," January 30, 2024, https://www.psychiatry.org/news-room/news-releases/new-apa-poll-one-in-three-americans-feels-lonely-e

3 Milena Batanova, Richard Weissbourd, and Joseph McIntyre, *Loneliness in America: Just the Tip of the Iceberg?* (Cambridge, MA: Making Caring Common, Harvard Graduate School of Education, October 2024), https://mcc.gse.harvard.edu/reports/loneliness-in-america-2024

4 University of Florida, Bureau of Economic and Business Research, *Social Isolation in America: Changes in Core Discussion Networks* (Gainesville, FL: University of Florida, n.d.), https://bebr.ufl.edu/sites/default/files/Social%20Isolation%20in%20America%20Changes%20in%20Core.pdf

5 Patrick C. Arp et al., "Replication Study: Predictors of Loneliness in U.S. Adults Over Age Sixty-Five," University of Pennsylvania, Population Center Working Paper, 2025, https://repository.upenn.edu/server/api/core/bitstreams/e0891fde-37aa-4b4e-8941-897979d5c0cf/content.

6 Christos Pezirkianidis et al., "Adult Friendship and Wellbeing: A Systematic Review with Practical Implications," *Frontiers in Psychology* 14 (2023): 1059057, https://doi.org/10.3389/fpsyg.2023.1059057

7 Julianne Holt-Lunstad, Timothy B. Smith, and J. Bradley Layton, "Social Relationships and Mortality Risk: A Meta-analytic Review," *PLOS Medicine* 7, no. 7 (2010): e1000316, https://doi.org/10.1371/journal.pmed.1000316.

8 Nancy E. Newall, Judith G. Chipperfield, Rodney A. Clifton, Raymond P. Perry,

Audrey U. Swift, and Joelle C. Ruthig, "Causal Beliefs, Social Participation, and Loneliness among Older Adults: A Longitudinal Study," *Journal of Social and Personal Relationships* 26, nos. 2–3 (2009): 273–90, https://doi.org/10.1177/0265407509106718

9 Marianne H. R. Scholte, Wilma A. M. Engels, Rutger C. M. E. de Kemp, and Jan Overbeek, "Social Reaction Styles, Interpersonal Behaviours and Person Perception: A Multi-Informant Approach," *Journal of Social and Personal Relationships* 16, no. 3 (1999): 315–33, https://doi.org/10.1177/0265407599163003

SLEEP

10 Stephen T. Wiebe et al., "Sleep Patterns and the Risk for Unipolar Depression: A Review," *Chronobiology International* 29, no. 6 (2012): 745–62, https://pmc.ncbi.nlm.nih.gov/articles/PMC3630972/.

11 Rachel Tompa, "How Sleep Affects Mental Health (and Vice Versa): What the Science Says," *Stanford Medicine*, August 11, 2025, https://med.stanford.edu/news/insights/2025/08/sleep-mental-health-connection-what-science-says.html.

12 Benjamin Zablotsky et al., "Associations Between Screen Time Use and Health Outcomes Among US Teenagers," *Preventing Chronic Disease* 18 (2021): 200573, https://www.cdc.gov/pcd/issues/2021/20_0573.htm

13 Francesco Salfi et al., "Effects of Total and Partial Sleep Deprivation on Reflection Impulsivity and Risk-Taking in Young Adults," *Nature and Science of Sleep* 12 (2020): 1175–83, https://pmc.ncbi.nlm.nih.gov/articles/PMC7261660/

14 Paola Zaninotto, George B. Ploubidis, and James Nazroo, "Longitudinal Associations Between Loneliness, Social Isolation, and Sleep Disturbance in Older Adults," *Aging & Mental Health* 23, no. 12 (2019): 1630–37, https://pmc.ncbi.nlm.nih.gov/articles/PMC6622793/

15 David J. Weeks, J. M. Michela, and P. A. Peplau, "The Relation between Loneliness and Depression: A Structural Equation Analysis," *Journal of Personality and Social Psychology* 76, no. 2 (1999): 279–89, https://pubmed.ncbi.nlm.nih.gov/10329298/

16 Daneyal Arshad et al., "The Adverse Impact of Excessive Smartphone Screen-Time on Sleep Quality among Young Adults: A Prospective Cohort Study," *Sleep Science* 14, no. 4 (2021): 337–41, https://pmc.ncbi.nlm.nih.gov/articles/PMC8776263/.

17 Ari Shechter et al., "Blocking Nocturnal Blue Light for Insomnia: A Randomized Controlled Trial," *Journal of Psychiatric Research* 96 (2018): 196–202, https://pubmed.ncbi.nlm.nih.gov/29101797/.

18 Jenna L. Adams et al., "Social Isolation and Mental Health Outcomes: A Population-Based Study," *PLOS ONE* 15, no. 2 (2020): e0228756, https://doi.org/10.1371/journal.pone.0228756.

19 Mohammad A. Alnawwar et al., "The Effect of Physical Activity on Sleep Quality and Sleep Disorder: A Systematic Review," *Cureus* 15, no. 8 (2023): e43595.

20 Rasha A. Alfawaz et al., "The Recommended Amount of Physical Activity, Sedentary Behavior, and Sleep Duration for Health in Adults: A Review of Guidelines," *International Journal of Environmental Research and Public Health* 18, no. 15 (2021): 8013, https://pmc.ncbi.nlm.nih.gov/articles/PMC8388570/.

21 Danielle Pacheco, "The Best Temperature for Sleep," *Sleep Foundation*, last modified July 11, 2025, https://www.sleepfoundation.org/bedroom-environment/best-temperature-for-sleep

22 https://www.sleepfoundation.org/bedroom-environment/light-and-sleep

23 https://pmc.ncbi.nlm.nih.gov/articles/PMC5187651/#sec1-3

24 https://cdnsciencepub.com/doi/10.1139/apnm-2020-0032?url_ver=Z39.88-2003&rfr_id=ori:rid:crossref.org&rfr_dat=cr_pub%20%200pubmed

25 https://pmc.ncbi.nlm.nih.gov/articles/PMC5598771/#S28

26 Cleveland Clinic, "What You Should Know About the Relationship Between Oversleeping and Depression," June 12, 2020, https://health.clevelandclinic.org/what-you-should-know-about-the-relationship-between-oversleeping-and-depression.

SCREENS

27 Laura Silver, Aaron Smith, Courtney Johnson, Jingjing Jiang, Monica Anderson, and Lee Rainie, "Majorities Say Mobile Phones Are Good for Society, Even Amid Concerns About Their Impact on Children," Pew Research Center, March 7, 2019, https://www.pewresearch.org/internet/2019/03/07/majorities-say-mobile-phones-are-good-for-society-even-amid-concerns-about-their-impact-on-children/.

28 Sean M. Twenge, Gabrielle N. Martin, and W. Keith Campbell, "Decreases in Psychological Well-Being Among American Adolescents After 2012

and Links to Screen Time During the Rise of Smartphone Technology," *Computers in Human Behavior* 86 (2018): 148–59, https://doi.org/10.1016/j.chb.2018.04.027

29 Elyssa M. Barrick, Alixandra Barasch, and Diana I. Tamir, "The Unexpected Social Consequences of Diverting Attention to Our Phones," *Journal of Experimental Social Psychology* 101 (2022): 104344, https://psnlab.princeton.edu/sites/g/files/toruqf641/files/documents/Barrick_Barasch_Tamir_2022.pdf.
qf641/files/documents/Barrick_Barasch_Tamir_2022.pdf

30 Julianne Holt-Lunstad, Timothy B. Smith, and J. Bradley Layton, "Social Relationships and Mortality Risk: A Meta-analytic Review," *PLOS Medicine* 7, no. 7 (2010): e1000316, https://doi.org/10.1371/journal.pmed.1000316

31 Khristopher J. Brooks, "Mark Zuckerberg Accused of Having 'Blood on His Hands' in Hearing on Online Child Exploitation," *CBS News*, January 31, 2024, https://www.cbsnews.com/news/mark-zuckerberg-meta-x-child-exploitation/

32 American Psychological Association, "Teens Are Spending Nearly 5 Hours Daily on Social Media. What Does This Mean for Their Mental Health?," *Monitor on Psychology*, April 2024, https://www.apa.org/monitor/2024/04/teen-social-use-mental-health

33 Jean M. Twenge, Thomas E. Joiner, Megan L. Rogers, and Gabrielle N. Martin, "Increases in Depressive Symptoms, Suicide-Related Outcomes, and Suicide Rates Among U.S. Adolescents After 2010 and Links to Increased New Media Screen Time," *Clinical Psychological Science* 6, no. 1 (2018): 3–17, https://doi.org/10.1177/2167702617723376.

34 American Psychological Association, "Social Media Brings Benefits and Risks to Teens," *Monitor on Psychology*, September 2023, https://www.apa.org/monitor/2023/09/protecting-teens-on-social-media.

35 Ybarra, Michele L., Kimberly J. Mitchell, and Josephine D. Korchmaros, "National Trends in Exposure to Online Sexual Content and Sexual Solicitation among Youth," *Journal of Adolesce*

36 Amy Orben and Andrew K. Przybylski, "The Association Between Adolescent Well-Being and Digital Technology Use," *Journal of Youth Studies* 22, no. 7 (2019): 1–19, https://doi.org/10.1080/02673843.2019.1590851.

37 American Psychological Association, "Zuckerberg Claims Social Media Isn't Harmful to Mental Health—Here's What the Science Says," February 9,

2024, https://www.apa.org/news/press/op-eds/zuckerberg-social-media-harmful.

EXERCISE

38 Riccardo Codella et al., "Physical Inactivity and Depression: The 'Gloomy Dual' Phenomenon," *Frontiers in Psychiatry* 13 (2023): 9862474, https://pmc.ncbi.nlm.nih.gov/articles/PMC9862474/.

39 University College London, "Low Fitness Linked to Higher Depression and Anxiety Risk," November 11, 2020, https://www.ucl.ac.uk/news/2020/nov/low-fitness-linked-higher-depression-and-anxiety-risk.

40 Sophie E. Spitzer et al., "Loneliness and Its Association with Mental and Physical Health Outcomes: A Systematic Review and Meta-analysis," *Nature Human Behaviour* (2024), https://doi.org/10.1038/s41562-023-01769-6

41 Roberto Codella and Andrea Chirico, "Physical Inactivity and Depression: The 'Gloomy Dual' with Rising Costs in a Large-Scale Emergency," *International Journal of Environmental Research and Public Health* 20, no. 2 (2023): 1603, https://doi.org/10.3390/ijerph20021603.

42 World Health Organization, *Global Recommendations on Physical Activity for Health* (Geneva: World Health Organization, 2010), https://iris.who.int/server/api/core/bitstreams/d0972fd5-8f7d-4c87-b092-889e0f5f4618/content

43 Roberto Codella and Andrea Chirico, "Physical Inactivity and Depression: The 'Gloomy Dual' with Rising Costs in a Large-Scale Emergency," *International Journal of Environmental Research and Public Health* 20, no. 2 (2023): 1603, https://doi.org/10.3390/ijerph20021603.

44 University of Missouri Extension, "Walking Is the Best Medicine," June 27, 2018, https://extension.missouri.edu/news/walking-is-the-best-medicine

45 Roberto Codella and Andrea Chirico, "Physical Inactivity and Depression: The 'Gloomy Dual' with Rising Costs in a Large-Scale Emergency," *International Journal of Environmental Research and Public Health* 20, no. 2 (2023): 1603, https://doi.org/10.3390/ijerph20021603.

46 M. N. Hossain et al., "The Impact of Exercise on Depression: How Moving Makes You Feel Better," *Cureus* 16, no. 6 (2024): e11298280, https://pmc.ncbi.nlm.nih.gov/articles/PMC11298280/.

DIET

47 Gail B. Crawford et al., "Depressive Symptoms and Self-Reported Fast-Food Intake in Midlife Women," *Preventive Medicine* 52, no. 3–4 (2011): 254–57, https://pmc.ncbi.nlm.nih.gov/articles/PMC3062726/.

48 Almudena Sánchez-Villegas et al., "Association of the Mediterranean Dietary Pattern with the Incidence of Depression: The Seguimiento Universidad de Navarra/University of Navarra Follow-up (SUN) Cohort," *Archives of General Psychiatry* 66, no. 10 (2009): 1090–98, https://doi.org/10.1001/archgenpsychiatry.2009.129.

49 Cleveland Clinic, "Mediterranean Diet," last modified March 7, 2024, https://my.clevelandclinic.org/health/articles/16037-mediterranean-diet.

PURPOSE

50 Bihong Xiao, Ziqiang Xin, and Luxiao Wang, "COVID-19's Influence on Life History Strategy: Insights from Cross-Temporal Meta-analysis and Experimental Research," *Personality and Individual Differences* 219 (2024): 112505, https://doi.org/10.1016/j.paid.2023.112505.

51 Michael J. Kyron, Andrew C. Page, Wai Chen, Jaime Delgadillo, and Hanh Ngo, "Beyond Meaning in Life: How a Perceived Futility in Searching for Meaning in Life Predicts Suicidal Ideation," *Death Studies* (2025): 1–11, https://doi.org/10.1080/07481187.2025.2529281.

52 Alimujiang et al., "Association Between Life Purpose and Mortality Among US Adults Older Than 50 Years," *JAMA Network Open* 2, no. 5 (2019): e194270, https://doi.org/10.1001/jamanetworkopen.2019.4270.

53 Mikael Dehara et al., "Parenthood Is Associated with Lower Suicide Risk: A Register-Based Cohort Study of 1.5 Million Swedes," *Acta Psychiatrica Scandinavica* 143, no. 3 (2021): 206–15, https://doi.org/10.1111/acps.13240.

54 M. A. Alzahrani et al., "Lifestyle Factors and Mental Health Outcomes: A Comprehensive Review," *Healthcare* 13, no. 3 (2025): 3067, https://doi.org/10.3390/healthcare130303067.

55 Ryan E. Lawrence, Maria A. Oquendo, and Barbara Stanley, "Religion and Suicide Risk: A Systematic Review," *Archives of Suicide Research* 20, no. 1 (2016): 1–21, https://doi.org/10.1080/13811118.2015.1004494.

ABOUT SUICIDE

56 Centers for Disease Control and Prevention, "Facts About Suicide," last modified March 26, 2025, https://www.cdc.gov/suicide/facts/index.html

57 Saloni Dattani, Fiona Spooner, Hannah Ritchie, and Max Roser, "Causes of Death," *Our World in Data*, 2023, https://ourworldindata.org/causes-of-death.

HELPING

58 University of South Carolina, "Warning Signs of Suicide," https://sc.edu/about/offices_and_divisions/student-health-well-being/mental-health/suicide-prevention/warning-signs/

59 https://pmc.ncbi.nlm.nih.gov/articles/PMC3372684/#S13

60 https://www.nimh.nih.gov/health/publications/5-action-steps-to-help-someone-having-thoughts-of-suicide

61 https://pubmed.ncbi.nlm.nih.gov/15811983/

www.ingramcontent.com/pod-product-compliance
Lightning Source LLC
La Vergne TN
LVHW090328210926
848480LV00004B/1335
9798996193813